W9-BAO-060

Plains Indian Wars
UPDATED EDITION

SHERRY MARKER

JOHN S. BOWMAN
GENERAL EDITOR

®
Facts On File, Inc.

Note on Photos
Many of the illustrations and photographs used in this book are old,
historical images. The quality of the prints is not always up to modern
standards, as in some cases the originals are from glass negatives or are damaged.
The content of the illustrations, however, made their inclusion important
despite problems in reproduction.

Plains Indian Wars, Updated Edition
Copyright © 2003, 1996 by Sherry Marker
Maps pages 22, 44, 49, 61, 90, and 124–125 Copyright © 2003 Facts On File
Maps pages 7, 27, 32, and 115 Copyright © 2000 Carl Waldman
and Facts On File

Facts On File, Inc.
132 West 31st Street
New York NY 10001

Library of Congress Cataloging-in-Publication Data
Marker, Sherry.
Plains Indian wars / by Sherry Marker.—Updated ed.
p. cm. — (America at war)
Includes bibliographical references and index.
ISBN 0-8160-4931-9
1. Indians of North America—Wars—Great Plains—Juvenile literature.
2. Indians of North America—Wars—1815–1875—Juvenile literature.
I. Title. II. Series.
E78.G73 M36 2003
973.5—dc21   2002009556

Facts On File books are available at special discounts when purchased in bulk
quantities for businesses, associations, institutions, or sales promotions. Please call our
Special Sales Department in New York at (212) 967-8800 or (800) 322-8755.

You can find Facts On File on the World Wide Web at http://www.factsonfile.com

Text design by Erika K. Arroyo
Logo design by Smart Graphics
Maps by Jeremy Eagle

Printed in the United States of America

MP FOF 10 9 8 7 6 5 4 3 2 1

This book is printed on acid-free paper.

Contents

Preface

This book examines the long series of maneuvers, skirmishes, battles, massacres, treaties, and relocations that took place between about 1854 and 1900 and have come to be known as the Plains Indian Wars. Most U.S. wars have had a generally understood beginning and a definite end when peace was achieved. Settlers living on the eastern seaboard at the time of the American Revolution knew when hostilities broke out against the British in 1775 and quickly learned of the British surrender at Yorktown in 1781. Photographers and painters recorded the moment when Robert E. Lee surrendered to Ulysses S. Grant on April 9, 1865, at Appomattox Court House, marking the end of the Civil War. Older Americans vividly remember when the United States entered World War II after the Japanese attack on Pearl Harbor in 1941, and when victory was declared in Europe and in Japan in 1945.

The Plains Indian Wars were unusual in that they had no clear beginning and no clear end. Neither those who lived through the Plains Indian Wars nor historians studying the conflicts today agree precisely when the wars began, or when exactly they ended. There can even be some difference of opinion as to exactly which of the many Indian wars west of the Mississippi River deserve inclusion under the title "Plains Indian Wars." One thing that most historians now do agree on—and this is an important theme of this volume, one that elevates it beyond a mere recounting of battles—the Plains Indian Wars were the inevitable result of what the United States in the 19th century perceived as its "manifest destiny"—that is, settling the land between the Atlantic and Pacific Oceans. In order to accomplish this, it was necessary first to move west across the Mississippi, then to fight and subdue a widely diverse population of Native Americans in order to occupy their homelands. Some of these American Indians had already been pushed from their homes east of the Mississippi onto the Great Plains in the years leading up to the Plains Indian Wars. Others had lived there for as long as they—or anyone—could know.

This last point raises an issue that is only one of many that this book might not be able to examine in great detail but which some readers may wish to explore on their own. In recent years, many historians and archaeologists have attempted to determine just when the ancestors of the American Indians arrived in North America. To give an idea of the lack of certainty in answering this question, although this book accepts the prevailing scholarly view that the ancestors of the American Indians arrived in North America about 20,000 to 12,000 years ago, there are serious students of the subject who believe that the first peoples arrived in North America as early as 40,000 years ago. Still others would date the arrival of the ancestors of the North American Indians back even further—as far back as 200,000 B.C.

The reasons for such a divergence of opinion stem from the difficulties that even the most knowledgeable authorities face when attempting to study prehistory, the period before written records. Although constant progress is being made in the ability to date material remains, such as the bones of animals and humans, by radiocarbon and DNA analyses, archaeologists admit that in the absence of written records, much of what is known about the exact arrival time and the origins of the ancestors of the Native Americans remains uncertain.

Despite this, most scholars still agree that the so-called proto-Indians crossed from Asia into North America along what is known as the Bering Straits land bridge, which linked Asia and North America during the Ice Age until it disappeared some 10,000 years ago. Recent DNA studies support the long-standing assumption that most American Indians' ancestors arrived in North America from Siberia and Mongolia. Nonetheless, of late many scientists have been fascinated by DNA evidence that suggests that still other Native Americans—perhaps 3 percent—have DNA that indicates that their ancestors came from Europe.

Perhaps these ancestors of some American Indians had emigrated from Europe in a long series of transatlantic journeys, thousands of years before the *Mayflower* set sail. As one scholar, Smithsonian Institution anthropologist Dennis Stanford, has said, "They were from Iberia not Siberia." Most anthropologists who examine this DNA evidence, however, are inclined to believe that it simply means that there was some very early mixture of Caucasoid and Mongoloid peoples, whether while still in eastern Asia or after arriving in northwestern North America.

PREFACE

This controversy over the origins of the first Native Americans has focused a good deal of attention on the discovery in 1996 first of a skull, then of an almost complete skeleton, now known as Kennewick Man. The remains, found along the Columbia River, took its name from Kennewick, Washington, the town near which it was found. Almost immediately, Kennewick Man, thought to have lived some 9,200 years ago, was embroiled in controversy. Archaeologists and anthropologists, including James C. Chatters, who studied Kennewick Man, wanted the skeleton to be studied extensively to date it and determine its origin. Native Americans, led by members of the Nez Perce and Confederated Tribes of the Umatilla Reservation considered that removing a bone chip from Kennewick Man to study the DNA was sacrilegious; almost immediately, they sued for possession of what they regarded as ancestral remains. At present, the skeleton of Kennewick Man is in the Burke Museum in Seattle, awaiting a decision on its ultimate disposition and final resting place. In August 2002, Oregon federal judge John Jelderks ruled that scientists should be allowed to study the bones before reburial. Both sides vow to take the case all the way to the Supreme Court, if necessary. Those interested in keeping up on the developments with Kennewick Man might like to consult http://www.Kennewick-man.com.

Chatters himself thinks that the remains are not ancestral to the people who today regard themselves as Native American but are those of a member of a probably extinct Caucasoid people. Not surprisingly, most contemporary Native Americans deny this claim. This is not merely a scholarly controversy, but one that could have wide-ranging political implications: If contemporary Native Americans are descendants of but one of many immigrant groups who reached North America, their claim to be the continent's sole original inhabitants is no longer secure. There are many ramifications of the controversy over Kennewick Man, but whatever the outcome, it is hoped that this book will cause at least some people to pay closer attention to such issues.

Kennewick Man is but one of a number of recent cases involving the ancestors of contemporary American Indians—in particular, cases that are leading to the return of Indian skeletons or artifacts that were once routinely carried off to museums by even the most well-intentioned students of these cultures. In 1990 the Federal Native American Graves Protection and Repatriation Act was passed. This act required return of such human remains and associated articles.

In 2000, more than 2,000 skeletons that archaeologists brought first to Harvard University's Peabody Museum and then in part to Phillips Academy in Andover, Massachusetts, between 1915 and 1929 were returned for burial to the Pecos Pueblo in New Mexico. Studies of the Pecos Pueblo skeletons had already yielded important information on diet and disease. "Our ancestors have contributed significantly to science and the archaeological world," said Raymond Gachupin, governor of the Jemez Pueblo. Also in 2000, two 9,000-year-old skeletons known as Minnesota Woman and Brown's Valley Man were returned to the Dakota Sioux of Minnesota, even though the Dakota Sioux did not live in Minnesota 9,000 years ago. In addition, the Smithsonian Institution has returned a considerable portion of its holdings of Native American skeletal remains to a number of tribes. Many other remains in the Smithsonian's collection are of unknown origin, and one Smithsonian official, Thomas W. Killion, has suggested that a Tomb of the Unknown Indian be built near the new National Museum of the American Indian on the Mall in Washington, D.C. In Killion's words, "It could be the final resting place for one of the nameless Indians whose bones can never be repatriated, because we will never know what tribe he originally came from. Let one stand for all the rest."

Although passage and recent enforcement of the federal act has brought about return of many Native American remains and artifacts dedicated and left with bodies, many American Indians feel that their battle to reclaim human remains and artifacts from what they call the white American "vulture culture" has just begun. Indeed, many Native Americans think that it is irrelevant to know what tribe (as most non-Indians say) or nation (as most Indians say) any particular remains come from. These American Indians think that all such remains, even if they are what many scholars term "culturally unidentifiable" or "culturally unaffiliated," are their shared Native American ancestors.

The American Indian movement to reclaim human remains and artifacts is part of the growing trend among Native Americans and scholars of Native American history to "reclaim" the past for the American Indians. Recent studies, such as those contained in Philip DeLoria and Neal Salisbury's *Companion to American Indian History* (2001) look at issues from the standpoint of the American Indians, rather than looking at Native Americans as the "other," a marginalized population within the mainstream of U.S. history. The movement to study American Indian culture and history in and of itself, rather than in constant

PREFACE

reference to the dominant culture, is probably the most significant recent innovation in American Indian studies. This book cannot pretend to be other than it is, but it at least makes readers well aware of the warp and woof that various cultures—white Europeans, black African, and American Indian—have woven together to shape the history of the United States.

One important aspect of the reclaiming of Native American culture is the growing attempt to document and preserve as many as possible of the lost or soon-to-be lost American Indian languages. It is a sign of the progress made in this field that one of the prizewinning essays in the 2001 edition of the influential annual publication *Best American Essays* was Earl Shorris's "The Last Word." Shorris shows that 175 of the original 300 American Indian languages are still spoken today—but that all but 20 will soon be dead languages as the handful of elders who speak them die.

It is a pleasant irony that Shorris's essay, documenting the drive by Native American and other scholars to record these languages before they are lost forever, originally appeared in *Harper's*. *Harper's Weekly,* the ancestor of today's monthly magazine, was one of the first American publications to cover the Plains Indian Wars. Articles in *Harper's Weekly,* some illustrated by the marvelous draftsman and artist Frederic Remington, detailed the U.S. attempt to conquer and banish the Indians of the Great Plains and their culture. However sympathetic they may have been to some aspects of the Indians' culture, articles in *Harper's Weekly* and other publications extolled the virtues, for example, of Pennsylvania's Carlisle School, where entering Native American children were not only taught English but forbidden to speak a word of their own languages. Today, at schools such as the Red Cloud Indian School on the Lakota Sioux Pine Ridge Reservation, children have the opportunity to study the Lakota language.

Another recent work that has challenged conventional interpretation of the treatment of American Indians is Robert V. Remini's *Andrew Jackson and His Indian Wars* (2001). Remini suggests that Jackson's motives for relocating Indians west of the Mississippi were not genocidal but well-intentioned. In fact, Remini suggests, Jackson was motivated at least in part by the desire to find a new homeland for Indians who would otherwise have been killed as settlers moved west. Remini thinks that the fact that the Indian Removal Bill of 1830 merely delayed the destruction of these Indians, many of whom, he holds, died during the Plains Indian Wars, should not be held against Jackson. Needless to say, Remini's work has generated considerable controversy.

Advances in knowledge and changes in perception have touched even the bloodiest battlefields of the Plains Indian Wars. Recent archaeological discoveries have pinpointed the previously unknown site of the 1864 Sand Creek Massacre in Colorado. Descendants of the Southern Cheyenne who survived the massacre had preserved an oral tradition as to the battle site. In 1998, Chief Laird Cometsevah, with the help of Colorado senator Ben Nighthorse Campbell (himself Southern Cheyenne) pinpointed the exact location of the massacre. Cannonballs of the type used by the Colorado cavalry were found at the site, and the Southern Cheyenne's long oral tradition was vindicated. Campbell, with the support of the National Parks Conservation Association, put forward a recommendation that land be bought and designated as a national historic site. In October 2002 Congress approved it.

A significant result of the changing perceptions about—and held by—Native Americans occurred in 1991. In large part because of Indian lobbying, the former Custer Battlefield National Monument in Montana was renamed the Little Bighorn Battlefield National Monument. The new name is inclusive of all those who fought and died at the Battle of Little Bighorn in 1876—Plains Indian as well as U.S. Army soldiers. There has long been a memorial to George Armstrong Custer and the Seventh Cavalry on Last Stand Hill, but now there are plans to create a memorial to Custer's opponents: the Indians who fought there.

The title of a recent book by American Indian scholar Fergus Bordewich captures the dominant mood in Native American studies today: *Killing the White Man's Indian: Reinventing Native Americans at the End of the Twentieth Century* (1996). Bordewich quotes Indian lawyer Douglas Endreson as saying that "We are entering an era unlike any since the European arrival, when choices made by Indian tribes will determine the future." Endreson cites federal recognition of tribal rights, including the economically important right to establish and operate gaming (gambling) on tribal land. Not surprisingly, the establishment of gaming casinos as a result of the federal government's Indian Gaming Regulatory Act of 1988 has provoked considerable controversy. Many non-Indians are resentful at what they perceive as the Indian's unfair advantage in this lucrative sphere, and within the Native communities there are often fierce debates over whether the positive aspects of gaming outweigh the negative aspects.

PREFACE

For better or worse, by the year 2001, 201 of the 562 federally recognized Indian tribes were engaging in gaming—operating 321 gaming establishments in 29 states, employing 250,000 workers, and bringing in $10.6 billion (10 percent of the total gambling industry in the United States). With the exception of Utah, there are Indian-run gaming establishments in all the states where the Plains Indian Wars were fought.

It is clear, then, that scholars—and many other Americans—are rethinking virtually every aspect of Native American history and contemporary life. Much information is now available on the Internet at site such as:

www.nativeculture.com
www.hanksville.org/NAresources/
www.u.arizona.edu/~ecubbins/webcrit.html
www.nativeweb.org
www.indianz.com

In addition, most tribes (or Indian nations) and many important battle sites have websites, such as www.crystalinks.com/sioux.html.

This new updated edition has made an effort to reflect the changes in recent scholarship, and it hopes to motivate its readers to rethink certain conventional assumptions about this history. To this end, the new edition has added a series of mini-essays in boxes on important issues such as Native Americans as slaves and the "Lost Bird of Wounded Knee," both examples of the difficulties of assimilation in the 19th century. The greatly expanded bibliography includes works focusing on a wide range of Plains Indian studies, from the battlefields to today's reservations. The addition of a glossary of terms that many readers may be encountering for the first time should eliminate any protest that they do not know what a bustle looked like or what pemmican was. More maps help to fix the places discussed in their historical context and the added illustrations give a vivid sense of life in the years before and during the Plains Indian Wars. No single book can ever hope to capture the total reality of the experience of the Plains Indian, but this volume should provide an introduction and stimulate a desire to learn more.

1

A COW IS SHOT

In 1840, the American painter George Catlin looked back on the decade he had spent on the Great Plains painting portraits of Native Americans and scenes of their daily life. "I have visited forty-eight tribes," he wrote,

> the greater part of which I found speaking different languages and containing in all 400,000 souls. I have brought home safe and in good order, 310 portraits in oil, all painted in their native dress, and in their own wigwams; and also 200 other paintings in oil containing views of the villages—the wigwams—their games and religious ceremonies—their dances—their ball plays—their buffalo hunting and other amusements . . .

The Indians Catlin painted had the Great Plains almost to themselves except for the vast herds of buffalo—perhaps as many as 15 million—that provided meat for their diet and hides for their tipis and clothes. Some of these Indians had lived on the plains since long before Europeans came to North America. Others—including the Sioux and Comanche, so closely associated with the Greet Plains in today's popular imagination—had only migrated east onto the plains 100 years or so before Catlin's expedition.

A great many Indians and buffalo and a very few trappers and traders: this was what Catlin saw when he traveled west. Only a few trading posts along the Missouri and Mississippi Rivers dotted the plains; only the occasional steamboat run by the American Fur Company journeyed into the interior. In 1832, Catlin himself was a passenger on the

This painting by George Catlin, made during his travels through the West in the 1830s, portrays the artist in a humorous vein: Typically, a hunter would be chasing the buffalo! *(Library of Congress)*

Yellowstone, the first steamboat to travel the Missouri. The one overland track across the Great Plains when Catlin traveled there was the Santa Fe Trail, running some 800 miles from Independence, Missouri, to Santa Fe, New Mexico.

At this time, most Americans regarded the Great Plains—the vast expanse stretching from Canada's Saskatchewan River Basin to central Texas and including all the land between the Mississippi River and the Rocky Mountains—as an uninhabitable desert suitable only for its Indian inhabitants. The continental heartland was first characterized as a worthless desert by the 16th-century Spanish explorers, who were disappointed when they found no gold in their wanderings, and who encountered only the nomadic Querecho and Teya Indians, ancestors of the Plains Apache. Lewis and Clark echoed these early reports on their trip west in 1804 after the Louisiana Purchase doubled the territory controlled by the United States. The land, they said, was "desert and barren."

A few years later, in 1820, U.S. Army major Stephen Long traveled extensively across the Great Plains and confirmed that the entire area was a "Great American Desert" totally "unfit for civilization." Long saw only one possible benefit in the wasteland: He thought that its very uselessness would discourage settlers from continuing their westward migration and, as he put it, "stretching the nation too thin." In Long's view the Great American Desert was best left to its nomadic Indian inhabitants.

Long's phrase—"Great American Desert"—seized the popular imagination and soon became the way the nation thought of the Great Plains. It did not take long for it to occur to the federal government in Washington that the "Great American Desert" west of the Mississippi might provide the ideal solution to an increasingly pressing problem: how could the United States take control of the rich agricultural land inhabited by Indians on the eastern flanks of the Mississippi River? As settlers had pressed west, first across the Appalachians, and then across the Ohio River, they had pushed the Indians ahead of them into then-unsettled land. But no land was staying unsettled very long, and in 1830 President Andrew Jackson signed the Indian Removal Act, designed to move Indians from the desirable land east of the Mississippi to the plains west of the river. By 1840, some 90,000 Native Americans had been relocated to the plains, joining an Indian population of more than 250,000 who already lived there.

Steamboats like this transport steamer on Tennessee River could be found on many rivers of the Midwest in the mid-1800s. *(National Archives)*

Sacajawea (Sacagawea)

SACAJAWEA, THE YOUNG SHOSHONE INDIAN WHO accompanied Lewis and Clark on part of their transcontinental expedition in 1804–06 is probably the most famous Indian woman in American history. Despite her fame, it is not known when she was born or when she died. She seems to have been born sometime between 1784 and 1787 and may have died as early as 1812, or as late as 1884. Even her name is uncertain: was it Sacajawea ("Boat Launcher") or Sacagawea ("Bird Woman")? This much seems clear: she was born into the Shoshone tribe, captured by the Hidatsa, and sold to the French Canadian trapper Toussaint Charbonneau. Along with Charbonneau, their infant child Pomp strapped to her back, she journeyed west with Lewis and Clark, sometimes serving as their interpreter and thus helping to guide them. Despite this, Meriwether Lewis spoke slightingly of her, saying she would be happy anywhere if she had "enough to eat and a few trinkets." William Clark seemed to recognize her value in dealing with the Indian tribes the expedition encountered when he said, "A women with a party of men is a token of peace."

It seemed an excellent solution to the problem: move the eastern Indians into the "back of beyond" west of the Mississippi and let them share the land with the tribes already there. Why, after all, would any settlers ever want to live in the wasteland called the Great American Desert, much of which (including most of present-day Arizona, Nevada, Utah, New Mexico, Texas, and parts of Wyoming and Colorado) belonged to Mexico. And as for the land beyond the Great Desert, Mexico also held California, while the British held the Oregon territory. Consequently, the Pacific coast was of little interest to most Americans. All this made the barren grassland west of the Mississippi the logical place to resettle the Indians: outside the borders of the settled United States, as a handy buffer between the United States and the foreign powers to the south and west.

Then, everything changed. In 1845, Texas joined the Union; the next year, the British ceded the Oregon territory to the United States; and in 1848, as a result of the U.S.-Mexican War, Mexico handed over California and the rest of the Southwest. Suddenly, the western frontier of the inhabitable United States was no longer the Mississippi, but the Pacific Ocean itself. The west coast had land rich in timber in the Pacific Northwest, with the potential for fertile farmland in California—land rich also in the gold that would soon be discovered in California in 1848.

The gold rush was just that: Prospectors and settlers streamed west along the Santa Fe Trail and a new trail that ran directly through the

Westward Ho!
THE TRAILS THAT LED WEST

THE FIRST EXPLORERS WHO HEADED WEST FOLLOWED Indian trails as best they could. If they were lucky, as Lewis and Clark were, they had Indian guides, such as Sacajawea (Sacagawea), to assist them. As settlers began to head west, an elaborate network of trails was carved from the Missouri and Mississippi Rivers to the Pacific. The wagon trains filled with would-be settlers gathered in such towns as Independence and Kansas City, Missouri, and then set off westward. Some 40 miles out of Independence, the wagons either continued west or headed south, along the Santa Fe Trail, to Council Grove and Dodge City, Kansas, and on into New Mexico. The first group of traders and potential settlers journeyed from Missouri to New Mexico in 1822; in following years, the journey usually took about 40 to 60 days, if made in early summer, when the weather was favorable. In 1847, the first group of Mormons (Latter-day Saints) arrived in Salt Lake City, Utah, along what came to be known as the Mormon trail. The best known of the trails was the Oregon Trail (also called the Overland Trail), which wound its way across prairies and over mountains between Missouri and the Columbia River in the Oregon Territory. In fact, the Oregon Trail was not one but several different trails. The first successful journey with wagons from Missouri all the way to Oregon took place in 1842. The next year, some 900 settlers with more than 1,000 head of cattle journeyed together along the trail in what was known as the Great Migration. The 2,000-mile journey west usually took six months, and the last wagon train to use the trail did so in 1870. So many wagons passed along the trail that wagon ruts, cut into the ground, can still be seen, visible signs of the settlers who fulfilled America's "Manifest Destiny" to settle the entire continent from the Atlantic to the Pacific.

buffalo hunting grounds of the Plains Indians. This was known as the Oregon Trail, extending from the Missouri River west to the Columbia River territory in the Pacific Northwest. In 1842, 100 settlers headed west along the new trail. A year later, 1,000 traveled it, and after that, no one kept count. The concept of Manifest Destiny—the country's right to extend from coast to coast—had arrived.

The term *manifest destiny* was coined in 1845 by journalist John O'Sullivan to describe the growing belief that the United States had a right to push its boundaries west to the Pacific. In an article in the *United States Magazine and Democratic Review,* O'Sullivan—echoing public opinion—wrote that it was the "will of Heaven" for the United States to fulfill its "manifest destiny to overspread the continent" from the Atlantic to the Pacific. Most Americans believed that Manifest Destiny was, as one congressman put it, the "destiny of the Anglo-Saxon race." Relatively few Americans, among them the African-American leader Frederick Douglass, argued that Manifest Destiny was simply a fancy name for "land hunger." It was the belief in Manifest Destiny that led to the U.S. attempts to purchase California and Texas from Mexico,

This 19th-century engraving depicts fur trappers and traders under attack by Indians in the American West. Such confrontations were undeniably an "occupational hazard" as whites intruded on Indian territory and resources. *(Library of Congress)*

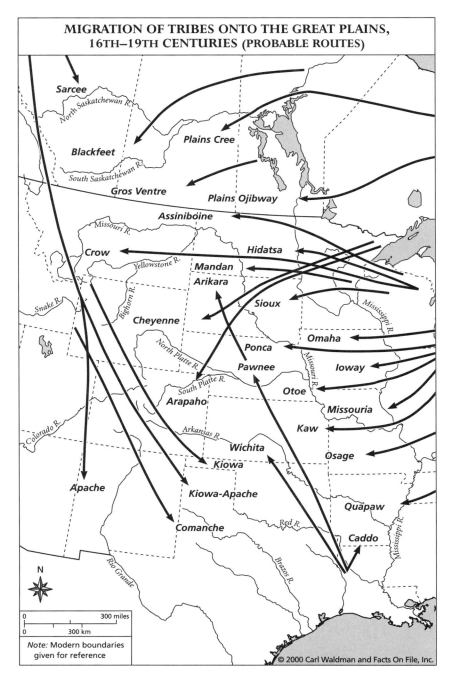

MIGRATION OF TRIBES ONTO THE GREAT PLAINS, 16TH–19TH CENTURIES (PROBABLE ROUTES)

Sarcee

North Saskatchewan R.

Plains Cree

Blackfeet

South Saskatchewan R.

Gros Ventre

Plains Ojibway

Assiniboine

Missouri R.

Crow

Yellowstone R.

Hidatsa

Mandan

Arikara

Snake R.

Bighorn R.

Cheyenne

Sioux

Mississippi R.

North Platte R.

Ponca

Omaha

Pawnee

Ioway

South Platte R.

Missouri R.

Otoe

Arapaho

Missouria

Colorado R.

Arkansas R.

Kaw

Wichita

Osage

Kiowa

Apache

Kiowa-Apache

Quapaw

Comanche

Red R.

Caddo

N

Rio Grande

Brazos R.

Mississippi R.

0   300 miles

0   300 km

Note: Modern boundaries
given for reference

© 2000 Carl Waldman and Facts On File, Inc.

the annexation of Texas in 1845, and the U.S.-Mexican War (1845–48), which brought Texas and California into the Union. And, in a very real sense, the belief in Manifest Destiny and the "destiny of the Anglo-Saxon race" made the Plains Indian Wars inevitable.

With the opening of the Santa Fe and Oregon Trails, the U.S. government found itself having to face a problem it thought had been solved: What to do with the Indians? In the early summer of 1851, the government in Washington ordered Indian agent Thomas Fitzpatrick to get word out to the many tribes living on the plains that they should come on September 1 to a great council at Fort Laramie, in southeast Wyoming, the halfway point on the Oregon Trail. Some tribes arrived almost at once; others arrived only in late August, but by September 1 as many as 12,000 Plains Indians from a wide variety of tribes, including the Sioux (Dakota, Lakota, Nakota), Northern Cheyenne, Arapaho, and Crow, had set up their camps outside the fort. After three weeks of debate, all the different tribes agreed to live on specific tribal lands and not to interfere with the traffic along the Oregon Trail. In return, the U.S. government promised to pay the Indians an annuity of $50,000 for 50 years. The payment, to be shared by all the different tribes, would not actually be in cash but in food and goods. To collect the annuity, the Indians would have to return each year to Fort Laramie.

For a while, the new system seemed to work, but in 1854, not far from Fort Laramie, a seemingly trivial incident broke the peace. Unlike most wars in which the United States has fought, the half-century of conflict that historians call the Plains Indian Wars did not begin with a formal declaration of war or a specific incident. But it just may have begun with a Mormon settler's cow.

At the same time that American Indians who lived east of the Mississippi were being pushed west against their wishes, a group of white settlers was sharing the same fate. The Mormons, followers of Joseph Smith, who founded the Church of Jesus Christ of Latter-day Saints in 1830, had to flee religious intolerance first in Ohio and then in Illinois, where Smith was murdered by a mob in 1844. After Smith's death, his successor, Brigham Young, decided to lead the Mormons west and find safety from persecution by settling on land that no one else wanted. Young chose the barren land around the Great Salt Lake in Utah, where Salt Lake City was founded in 1847. In the next years, more and more Mormons moved west along the Oregon Trail, then branched off onto the Mormon Trail to Salt Lake City itself.

A COW IS SHOT

A caravan of Mormons makes its way west during the mid-19th century. However idealistic and peaceable their motives, the Mormons were also moving onto and taking possession of Indian land. *(National Archives)*

In the late summer of 1854, considerable numbers of Indians, including a great number of Sioux (Dakota, Lakota, and Nakota), were camped near Fort Laramie, waiting for the distribution of their annual payment. Indian agent Thomas Fitzpatrick, who knew the area well, reported serious hunger and hardship among the Indians—due, in large part, to the fact that the heavy traffic along the Oregon Trail was driving away their main source of food, the buffalo. On August 18, yet another Mormon wagon train was making its way west toward Fort Laramie along the Oregon Trail. According to some accounts, a cow led by one of the Mormon pioneers was shot by an Indian. According to other reports, a hungry Indian simply happened on a lost cow and shot it for food. Whatever really happened, when the Mormons reached Fort Laramie, they reported that Indians had killed one of their cows—and word got back to the Sioux camp that there had been an altercation.

According to most versions of what happened, the Sioux chief Brave Bear went almost at once to Fort Laramie to offer amends for the cow.

Brave Bear suggested to the post commander, Lieutenant Fleming, that the matter of reparations be put before the Indian agent when he arrived to distribute the annuity. Lt. J. L. Grattan, a recent West Point graduate, argued against delay. Grattan pointed out that there had been other incidents in which Sioux had harassed settlers passing along the trails west. Perhaps the Indians needed to be taught a lesson. Grattan, who boasted that he could whip the "whole Sioux nation" with a few good men, asked to be allowed to settle the matter.

Grattan convinced Lieutenant Fleming to act, and was ordered to lead a party of U.S. cavalry to the Sioux camp and arrest the man who had shot the cow. With 27 infantrymen, two officers, an interpreter, and two small howitzers, Grattan set off, stopping to pick up French trader James Bordeaux at his trading post near the fort. About four miles out of Fort Laramie, Grattan and his party arrived at Brave Bear's camp, where several hundred Sioux were settled. Once again, Chief Brave Bear argued that the issue should be resolved by the Indian agent, who would arrive any day. Brave Bear felt that the matter was inconsequential and that High Forehead, who had shot the cow, should not be arrested. Brave Bear offered Grattan several ponies to make up for the loss of the cow, but Grattan was determined to arrest High Forehead and take him back to Fort Laramie.

Tempers began to rise and matters were not helped when Grattan's interpreter taunted the Sioux and assured them that the U.S. soldiers were looking forward to killing them and eating their hearts. High Forehead stood unarmed in front of his lodge and announced that he would rather be killed on the spot than arrested and imprisoned at Fort Laramie.

Suddenly, shots rang out—whose, nobody knows. Did the Sioux fire first, or was it one of Grattan's soldiers? Within minutes, both Sioux Chief Brave Bear and Lt. Grattan were wounded. As the soldiers attempted to flee back to Fort Laramie, the Sioux warriors pursued them, killing all but one. When the surviving soldier and French trader James Bordeaux got word of what had happened back to Fort Laramie, the soldiers there called it a "massacre." More accurately, this was just the latest in the long chain of misunderstandings between settlers and Indians that led to the final round of fighting we know as the Plains Indian Wars. When it all ended, some 50 years later, the paintings George Catlin had made to show how the Plains Indians lived would instead be a record of a vanished way of life.

2

FROM JAMESTOWN TO FORT LARAMIE

Two Centuries of Conflict

The Plains Indian Wars are only the last chapter in the history of conflict between the American Indians and the European settlers that began almost as soon as the first European stepped ashore in North America. Conflict between the American Indians and the steady stream of settlers who poured into their homelands between the 16th and 19th century was virtually inevitable for a simple reason: what the Europeans saw as a sparsely populated and uncivilized "New World" ripe for conquest and settlement, the Indians saw as their ancestral homeland. The remark of one early English settler neatly sums up the basic European view toward the New World: "It is lawful now to take a land which none useth and make use of it."

To the Europeans, land without settlements, towns, and cities was by definition undeveloped, unused land. It was land to be acquired, owned, and developed. The Indian view was quite different: Individual ownership of land was a foreign concept to the Indians, who did, nonetheless, accept that different tribes had generally accepted rights to hunt, fish, and farm certain areas. Tribal warfare often broke out when one tribe attempted to drive a weaker tribe off land that custom, not ownership, made its own.

That buying and selling land was incomprehensible to the Indians led to repeated misunderstanding over treaties. The Indians thought a treaty simply extended to the European newcomers the right to share

Spanish explorer Hernando De Soto explored the Mississippi River in 1541. *(Library of Congress, Prints & Photographs Division [LC-D418-9874])*

the land, while the Europeans thought that they gained permanent, exclusive ownership of Indian land through treaties. The pejorative phrase "Indian giver," meaning someone who first gives something away and then takes it back, reflects this profound misunderstanding.

Hindsight makes it easy to see almost all the elements of the long struggle between settlers and Indians in the history of the first permanent English settlement, founded in Jamestown, Virginia, in 1607. One of the first Jamestown settlers, a Master George Perch, wrote that his companions were "almost ravished" by their first sight of Chesapeake Bay. The Powhatan Indians, led by Chief Wahunsonacock, whom the English simply called "Powhatan," sometimes helped and sometimes attacked the newcomers. When Powhatan's daughter Pocahontas converted to Christianity and married tobacco merchant John Rolphe, tensions temporarily eased. Nonetheless, in 1622, the Indians attacked Jamestown and its outlying settlements and killed a number of settlers. Many of those slain were left with their mouths stuffed with dirt as a warning that survivors should not "eat" Indian land. The colonists of course, regarded this not as a pointed message but an act of savagery.

Despite pestilence and hardship, Jamestown had 8,000 settlers by 1644. As Jamestown grew, it absorbed more and more Indian land where the colonists planted tobacco for the profitable export trade. The Indians, who had thought initially that the settlers only wanted enough land to live on and farm for their own needs, saw great tracts of their hunting grounds disappearing under cultivation.

In 1644, the Indians made one last attempt to drive out the Jamestown settlers, failed, and retreated in the hope that the settlers would not follow. Their hopes were short-lived. By the time of the American Revolution, virtually all of Virginia had been colonized—and the Powhatan had virtually disappeared from the land that had been their home for so long.

The history of Jamestown, then, presaged much of what was to come: The Indians did not realize soon enough that the settlers wanted land not just to live on but to exploit for profit. In Jamestown, the land was wanted for tobacco. In the next 250 years, other land would be mined for gold, stripped for timber, cleared for farmland, and bisected for railroads. In Indian eyes, the settlers did "eat" the land. The settlers, of course, saw it differently: they were civilizing a wilderness and

This depiction of American Indians conducting a sacrificial harvest ceremony, widely circulated in 16th-century Europe, was typical of images that encouraged Europeans to believe that the Indians were exotic savages. *(Library of Congress)*

This photograph is of the painting by Richard Norris Brooke of Pocahontas during her stay in England. *(Library of Congress, Prints & Photographs Division [LC-D416-151])*

converting the Indians, whom many devout settlers viewed as "children of Satan," to Christianity.

At about the same time that the Powhatan were being pushed out of their homeland in Virginia, the Pequot of the Connecticut River Valley were driven from their homelands in the Pequot War of 1637. In the following years, the New England Indians were repeatedly pushed off their land as the settlers advanced. Then, in 1675–76, Metacomet, a Wampanoag Indian chief known to the settlers as King Philip, attempted to stem the tide. King Philip and his forces, whom the clergyman Increase Mather called "devils of desperation," attacked settlements throughout New England. After the last great battle of the war near Kingston, Rhode Island, in August of 1676, Philip and many of his people were dead and the Indians of southern New England had effectively been eradicated. Most of the surviving Indians were sold into slavery in the southern colonies and the West Indies, a pattern often repeated in the years to come.

The English, of course, were not the only Europeans interested in colonizing the New World. Two other large groups of European colonists—the Spanish and the French—took different approaches to relations with the Native population. By and large, the French, interested more in the lucrative fur trade than in creating settlements, moved among and worked with the Indians, but did not push them

Metacomet, or King Philip, became chief of the Wampanoag in 1662. *(Library of Congress, Prints & Photographs Division [LC-USZ62-96234])*

from their land. The French established a string of trading posts in Canada and then, under Père Marquette and René-Robert de La Salle, explored the Mississippi and claimed the land they called Louisiana for France in 1682. The vast Louisiana territory—containing most of the future states of Louisiana, Arkansas, Missouri, Kansas, Iowa, Minnesota, Oklahoma, Kansas, Colorado, Nebraska, Wyoming, North and South Dakota, and Montana—was to pass between the French and Spanish before the United States finally purchased it from the French in 1803.

In the years immediately following Columbus's voyages of exploration (1492–1502), the Spanish were most interested in exploring and exploiting Central and South America. Then, Spanish explorers began to scout out the territory north of Mexico, concentrating their efforts on the Atlantic coast between Georgia and Florida and California; in addition, they explored much of the Southwest (the future states of Arizona and New Mexico and parts of Texas, Utah, and Nevada), as well as parts of what would become Kansas, Oklahoma, and Nebraska. In 1540, the Spanish explorer Don García López de Cárdenas was the first European to see the Grand Canyon. In fact, the first permanent European settlement in North America was Spanish Saint Augustine, founded in Florida in 1565.

As Spain attempted to extend its New World empire north from Mexico, important mission settlements were built at Santa Fe, New Mexico, in 1610; El Paso, Texas, in 1682; and Tucson, Arizona, in 1700. Between 1769 and 1776, a string of missions was built in California, from San Diego in the south to San Francisco in the north.

By and large, as they moved north of Mexico, the Spanish subdued, but did not expel, the native population. Often the Spaniards moved entire tribes onto their missions, converted them to Christianity, and tried to instruct them in European ways. Disease and hardship took their toll: California's Indian population dropped from an estimated 310,000 Indians in 1769 when the San Diego mission was founded to half that number in 1834.

Just as individual groups of settlers and Indians came into conflict, so, too, did competing groups of Europeans. For much of the period of 1689–1763, the great European powers were engaged in hostilities in Europe and elsewhere around the world. Inevitably, these hostilities spilled over into the New World. Equally inevitably, the Indians were drawn into those conflicts: both the French and English, for example, competed for favor with the powerful Iroquois League—composed of

Missionaries Among the Indians

ALMOST FROM THE BEGINNING, EUROPEAN SETTLERS in the New World tried to convert Native Americans to Christianity. Perhaps the most ambitious missionaries were the Jesuit and Franciscan priests sent by Spain into the Southwest and California. By the late 1500s, Catholic missionaries had converted people in much of what is now New Mexico. By the late 1700s, a string of missions ran the length of California from San Diego to San Francisco and had spread into parts of the Great Plains. French Catholic missionaries built missions with schools to educate Indian children in Quebec and also traveled west with fur trappers and traders, spreading the gospel as they made their way also in the Great Plains. By the 1640s, the Puritans in Massachusetts had established 14 so-called Praying towns for Indian converts. Throughout the 19th century, Protestant missionaries, including many Methodists and Presbyterians, established mission schools among the Indians throughout the West. Indeed, the first European-American women to cross the Rockies, Narcissa Whitman and Eliza Spalding, journeyed to the Pacific coast in the 1830s along with their missionary husbands.

This activity was carried out by devoted, idealistic Christians, but they were often insensitive at best and cruel at worst in their dealings with the Native Americans. At one extreme were the Spanish missions in the Southwest and on the West Coast; although often portrayed as oases of happy souls, these missions often worked the Indians extremely hard and harshly punished those who resisted or "strayed." Uprisings and rebellions were not uncommon, the best-known being that of the Pueblo Indians (1680–96). At the other extreme were the efforts of the Quakers, who were less insistent on proselytizing and more interested in improving the Indians' lives. By the 1830s, Quakers were establishing schools among the Shawnee in Kansas; in the 1870s, Quakers in Texas tried to prevent what became the Red River War. Between these two extremes were the many missionaries throughout the West—both Protestant and Catholic—who exerted themselves with a genuine regard for the Indians, but who nevertheless had little or no respect for their indigenous religion and culture.

the Mohawk, Oneida, Onondaga, Cayuga, Seneca and, after 1722, Tuscarora Indians. The Iroquois League sided with the British during most of the French and Indian Wars, but was divided in its loyalties during the American Revolution. In 1733, when James Oglethorpe founded the colony of Georgia as an English outpost against the Spanish, the Creek Indians promised "to give no encouragement to any other white people to settle among us." In Arkansas, a few years later, the English and French both wooed local Creek and Chickasaw.

Finally, between 1754 and 1763, many Indian tribes sided with either the English or the French during the last phase of the French and Indian Wars (known in Europe as the Seven Years' War). When it was over, the English held Canada and the United States as far west as the Mississippi. The French had lost their North American empire and the Indians had lost their French allies. As for the Spanish, they held New Orleans and the vast region west of the Mississippi known as the Louisiana Territory, including much of present-day Louisiana, Arkansas, Oklahoma, Missouri, Kansas, Colorado, Iowa, Nebraska, Minnesota, North and South Dakota, Wyoming, and Montana. In addition, the Spanish held Texas, California, much of the Southwest, including Texas, New Mexico, Arizona, Nevada, and Utah.

In October of 1763, in the Proclamation of 1763, the British forbade any settlement west of the Appalachians. By so doing, they hoped to mollify the Indians, with whom they maintained a profitable trade in deerskins and fur, and to quell the outbreak of an Indian resistance movement. The proclamation was a failure, ignored both by Chief Pontiac and by the colonists, who continued to move west. Part Ottawa and part Chippewa, Pontiac was able to unite both tribes and to launch an all-out attempt to drive the English out of a wide swath of territory from Michigan to New York. Pontiac's initial success staggered the British: although Detroit withstood repeated attacks, Pontiac's forces destroyed a vital string of British military garrisons from Michigan to Niagara. By 1765, almost all the British frontier settlements had been destroyed except Detroit. Pontiac's failure to take that settlement caused many of his followers to lose heart and surrender to the British, although Pontiac himself fought on. Pontiac's Rebellion did not end until 1766 when, after a series of defeats, the chief and his remaining followers surrendered to the English at Oswego, New York.

Pontiac's defeat left other tribes disheartened, and in 1768, at Fort Stanwix on the Mohawk River, the Iroquois ceded their extensive holdings in what are now southwestern New York, western Pennsylvania, West Virginia, Kentucky, and Tennessee to the British. In return, the English attempted to reassure the Indians that their remaining territory

Throughout the American Revolution, Mohawk leader Joseph Brant supported the British in their fight against the Americans. *(Library of Congress, Prints & Photographs Division [LC-USZ62-20488])*

would be spared new settlement. But it was too late. Already colonists had moved, and would continue to move, into Indian lands, including the lands west of the Alleghenies, the western range of the Appalachian Mountains, where Daniel Boone explored parts of Kentucky in 1769. In the following years, settlers poured across the Appalachians: in 1780, there were only 2,000 settlers west of the mountains; 10 years later, 100,000 settlers had crossed the Appalachians.

During the American Revolution, both the English and the colonials wooed the Indians, seeking their support, or at least their neutrality, in the conflict. In 1775, the Continental Congress asked the Indians essentially to mind their own business and regard the war as a "family quarrel" of no importance to them. Many Indians, including the Iroquois, Algonquians, and Cherokee, sided with the British, who promised to respect their homelands if they defeated the colonials.

Three years later, in 1778, the Continental Congress authorized its first treaty with the Indians in an attempt to convince the Lenni Lenape (Delaware) Indians to stand against the British. For their cooperation, the Lenni Lenape (Delaware) were promised their own state when the United States gained its independence, and full congressional representation. After independence, Congress ignored the treaty entirely.

Under the terms of the Peace of Paris of 1783, which formally ended the American Revolution, the United States took possession of the continent up to the Mississippi, the Spanish received Florida, and the English retained Canada. A year later, the Confederation Congress passed legislation attempting to "restrain" its citizens from "further trespass" on Cherokee land. The new nation's citizens ignored their government and continued to move west. Some even threatened to secede from the new country and create a new nation, an idea which horrified Congress.

In 1787, Congress recognized the continued westward movement by passing the Northwest Ordinance, which provided for the orderly settlement of the vast Ohio Territory, bounded by the Ohio River, the Great Lakes, and the Mississippi, without regard to the Indian population. According to the terms of the Northwest Ordinance of 1787, land was to be developed into between three and five territories, which would be officially recognized once each had a population of 5,000 male settlers. When a territory had 60,000 citizens, it could apply for statehood, as Ohio did in 1803. In the years immediately after the passage of the Northwest Ordinance, the British supported the Indians in their stand against the new settlers, but soon withdrew significant support. Consequently, the Indians ceded most of their land in the Northwest Territory to the Americans in the Treaty of Fort Greenville in 1795.

In 1803, the United States doubled its size when it purchased the Louisiana Territory from France. At the same time, the United States eliminated France from its borders. Now only Spain stood between the new nation and the Pacific Ocean. As Lewis and Clark explored the Louisiana Territory and pushed west to the Pacific, settlers and fur traders rushed into the territory: by 1812, some 70,000 had settled there.

The United States was steadily moving west, pushing the Indians out of their territories, just as the first settlers had done. But while the settlers had acted unofficially, now the U.S. government began to develop what would become a national policy of removing the Indians from their land and resettling them. After the Louisiana Purchase of 1803,

This early 19th-century drawing depicts Lewis and Clark addressing a group of Indians encountered on their expedition of 1804–06. Lewis and Clark encouraged the view that white people could deal reasonably and peaceably with the Indians, but few whites shared their opinion. *(Library of Congress)*

President Jefferson proposed to Congress that all Indians remaining east of the Mississippi be moved west of the river onto the newly acquired land. Although Congress did not act on Jefferson's suggestion, the policy of removal would soon gain favor.

In 1812, the United States declared war on Great Britain, in part because the English were encouraging Indians, including the powerful Shawnee chief Tecumseh, to harass settlements. Even before the War of 1812, Tecumseh had attempted, with limited success, to unite Indians against further encroachments on their land. Between 1808 and 1810, Tecumseh traveled widely, trying to persuade Indians as far south as the Seminole of Florida and as far east as the Iroquois of New York to join forces and live together in Indiana.

While Tecumseh was traveling, some of his people signed away their land to the new governor of the Indiana Territory, Gen. William Henry Harrison. Upon his return in 1810, Tecumseh met with Harrison at Vincennes, Indiana, to argue that the treaties by which Harrison had taken possession of Indian lands were invalid, because the land was held in joint possession by all Indians and could never be given away by treaty.

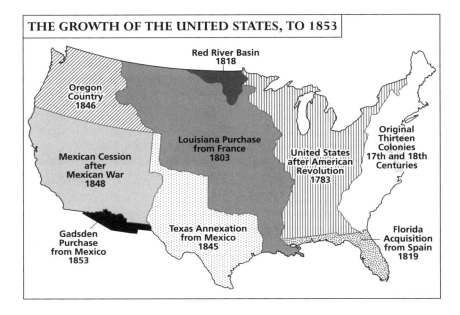

THE GROWTH OF THE UNITED STATES, TO 1853

Red River Basin
1818

Oregon
Country
1846

Louisiana Purchase
from France
1803

Mexican Cession
after
Mexican War
1848

United States
after American
Revolution
1783

Original
Thirteen
Colonies
17th and 18th
Centuries

Gadsden
Purchase
from Mexico
1853

Texas Annexation
from Mexico
1845

Florida
Acquisition
from Spain
1819

According to a story later attributed to Tecumseh himself, when Harrison and Tecumseh met, they sat side by side on a bench, and Tecumseh moved closer and closer to Harrison, who nervously moved away. Finally, as Harrison was about to topple off the bench, he protested that he had no room left. Tecumseh pointed out that he was only treating Harrison the way that white men were treating the Indians.

Not surprisingly, this is not the only account of this famous meeting. In his *Life of Tecumseh* (1841), Benjamin Drake, who claimed to base his version on the eyewitness account of a Captain Ford, says that Tecumseh pointedly refused to sit beside Harrison and insisted on sitting on the ground, which he called the "bosom of his mother."

Although the details of Harrison's meeting with Tecumseh are unclear, the results of the meeting are known: Harrison and Tecumseh could not reach an agreement. Tecumseh resorted to force, fighting with the British against the Americans until he was killed in 1813 near present-day Chatham, Ontario, at the Battle of the Thames, a decisive battle of the War of 1812.

Just as the Indians had earlier lost their French allies, now they had permanently lost their British allies. Now they stood alone against the Americans, who no longer needed to court them as allies against foreign powers. This, combined with the decline of the once-profitable fur trade, meant that the Americans no longer needed the Indians as allies or partners. What they needed was the Indians' land.

In the years immediately after the war, feisty former congressman and future president Andrew Jackson led U.S. forces in a number of victories against southeastern Indian tribes in the Creek War of 1813–14. In March 1814 Jackson soundly defeated the Creek under Chiefs Red Eagle and Red Sticks at the Battle of Horseshoe Bend. Jackson's enemies included most of the Indians whose literacy later led whites to call them the "Five Civilized Tribes": the Creek, Cherokee, Chickasaw, Choctaw, and Seminole. At the same time, the government's Indian removal policy continued. In 1814 and again in 1825, the Creek Indians of Alabama and Georgia, who had fought with Tecumseh against the Americans during the War of 1812, ceded portions of their land to the government, which ordered them to move west of the Mississippi into the land the U.S. government had designated as Indian Territory (roughly present-day Oklahoma and part of Kansas). Guarded by a string of forts, the Indian Territory was meant

Tecumseh, chief of the Shawnee, was killed during the Battle of the Thames on October 18, 1813. *(Library of Congress, Prints & Photographs Division [LC-USZ62-26050])*

to create what government officials called a "permanent Indian frontier," marking the division between Indian territory to the west and white settlement to the east.

In 1828, Andrew Jackson was elected president, and two years later Congress enacted the Indian Removal Act of 1830. According to the terms of the removal act, all previous treaties recognizing Indian rights to lands east of the Mississippi were null and void. The Indians were to leave their tribal homelands and move west of the Mississippi, primarily into the Indian Territory, where they would receive new land.

Although the removal act urged the Indians to move "voluntarily" and did not mandate the use of force, the federal government turned a

Native Americans as Slaves

ALTHOUGH NO TRIBE DEPENDED ON SLAVE LABOR, slavery was not unknown among most of the Indian tribes of North America. From the Kwakiutl Indians of the Pacific Northwest to the Sioux (Dakota, Lakota, and Nakota) of the Great Plains and the Pequot of New England, Native Americans enslaved other Indians whom they captured in raids. Some of these captives remained slaves; some were tortured and sacrificed to pacify the spirit of a departed family member who had been slain in battle; still others, especially women and children, were absorbed into their captors' tribe. When the European explorers and settlers arrived in North America, they soon realized the potential source of cheap labor in enslaving Indians. In contrast, the Indians of the Southwest and Great Plains used the Europeans whom they occasionally captured not for cheap labor but as a useful commodity to trade, often for ransom. Until slavery was outlawed in the United States, Native Americans were a valuable source of cheap labor: In 1708, one-third of all slaves in South Carolina were Native Americans, most from the Tuscarora tribe. Enslaved Indians were often exported to the Caribbean islands of the West Indies, where they worked alongside slaves imported from Africa. In the 18th century in Florida, slavers enslaved entire villages of Muskogee (Creek) and Tocobaga Indians. Some Indians in the South also owned African-American slaves, but later in the 19th century the Seminole of Florida welcomed and absorbed into their communities many African slaves who fled servitude.

blind eye to what happened next. In 1831–32, the Choctaw of Georgia, Louisiana, and Mississippi were forcibly removed to Oklahoma in the dead of winter. In 1834, the Chickasaw of Mississippi were also forced to move to Oklahoma. In 1836, U.S. troops rounded up some 20,000 Creek and forcibly marched them—many in chains—to the Indian Territory. Less than 100 years after the establishment of the Georgia colony, the powerful Creek Confederation of Alabama and Georgia, made up of some 50 tribes, was no more. Then, in 1837, the Ho-Chunk (Winnebago) of eastern Wisconsin were removed to western Wisconsin and Nebraska, although some managed to return home in following years.

The policy of removal also virtually eradicated the Cherokee—the largest single group of Indians living in the Southeast. After the Removal Act was passed in 1830, the Georgia Cherokee were hounded out of Georgia to Tennessee, where their chief, Kooweskoowe, known as John Ross, took their case to the courts. In 1832, in *Worcester v. Georgia*, the Supreme Court ruled that treaties assuring Cherokee rights to Georgia land were still valid, but when both federal and state governments ignored the ruling, Ross's victory was meaningless. In 1838, Ross had to lead his people on the forced march known as the "Trail of Tears." At least 4,000 of the 18,000 Cherokees whom Gen. Winfield Scott and his troops forced to march on foot during the bitter winter of 1838–39 died en route to the Indian Territory. U.S. Army interpreter John Burnett, who accompanied Scott, later wrote: "Murder is murder and somebody must answer . . . Somebody must explain the four-thousand silent graves that mark the trail of the Cherokees to their exile."

Matters were no better for the Florida Seminole, led by the notable chief Osceola. The Seminole almost immediately thought better of the treaty of removal they had signed in 1832 and fought removal during the Seminole War (1835–42). Many African-American slaves who had escaped to Seminole territory fought along with the Seminole. Finally, after a scorched-earth campaign had effectively destroyed their livelihood, the Seminole surrendered in 1842. Some managed to hide themselves deep within the Everglades, while most were removed to Oklahoma, with an estimated loss of 40 percent of their population. One who survived described their plight in Oklahoma, where they were "hungry, cold, and destitute" and trying to survive in "a cold climate."

This portrait of Osceola was drawn on stone by George Catlin, from his original portrait. *(Library of Congress, Prints & Photographs Division [LC-USZC2-3009])*

Between 1830, when the Indian Removal Act was signed, and 1850, some 90,000 Indians were removed from their homelands and relocated in the Indian Territory. The purpose of the removals was simple: to move Indians from the desirable rich farmland east of the Mississippi and settle them west of the river in the barren Great Plains, which U.S. Army major Stephen Long had called "the Great American Desert" when he traveled there in 1820.

In 1834, Congress legislated against settlement in the Indian territory. With both Mexico and England holding so much land west of the Mississippi, it was logical to assume that the Mississippi would remain the United States's western boundary. Beyond lay the Great Desert, with the vast British-held Oregon territory stretching from the Pacific to the Rocky Mountains and south to California. California, along with New Mexico, Arizona, Nevada, Utah, Texas, and parts of Colorado and Wyoming belonged to another foreign power, Mexico, which had gained

its independence from Spain in 1821. Yet by 1848, all of that vast territory had become part of the Union, pushing the western boundary from
the Mississippi to the Pacific and breaching the so-called "permanent
Indian frontier."

Soon the Great Desert was traversed by trails and roads leading to
the Oregon territory, whose rivers were rich in beavers and otters.
Among the early settlers were missionaries Narcissa Whitman and Eliza
Spalding, the first known white women to cross the continent (1836).
Along with their husbands, the two women were killed by the Cayuse
(Waiilatpu) Indians in 1847 after a devastating outbreak of measles
killed many of the local Indians. Not even the news of hostilities and
epidemics could deter the gold prospectors, trappers, and settlers in
Conestoga wagons who headed west across a network of trails, through
the land that Andrew Jackson had thought worthless enough to hand
over to the Indians in 1830. Instead, as the number of settlers increased,
the number of Indians was steadily eroded. In California, for example,
some 95,000 gold prospectors had set up shop by 1849. Initially, many
Indians worked in the mines, but improved mining techniques soon
diminished the need for cheap labor. By 1870, perhaps as few as 30,000
Indians were left in California.

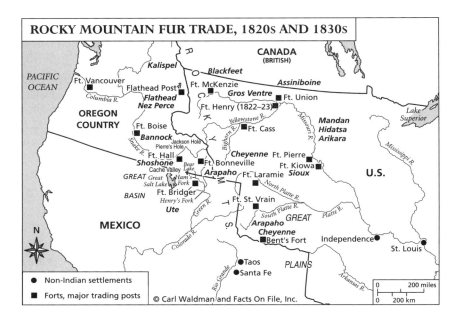

ROCKY MOUNTAIN FUR TRADE, 1820s AND 1830s

PLAINS INDIAN WARS

This mid-19th-century drawing depicts a caravan of immigrants crossing the South Platte River, Nebraska, as the Indians stand by and watch. Eventually the Indians would find that they were overwhelmed by the sheer volume of such immigrants. *(Library of Congress)*

By the mid-19th century, it was clear that the Indians of the Great Plains, and the Indians so recently relocated there in the removal acts, were an impediment to westward expansion as the United States followed its Manifest Destiny to the Pacific. Once more, as at every step of settlement and expansion, from the tobacco fields of Jamestown to the final push to the Pacific, conflict between the Indians and the settlers was inevitable. The last chapter of that conflict is the Plains Indian Wars.

3

THE GREAT PLAINS
AND ITS PEOPLE

Any account of how Native Americans came to live
on the Great Plains is part of the much larger story of how the Indians
first came to live in North America. In 1590, José de Acosta, a Spanish
Jesuit missionary to Peru, speculated in his book *The Natural and Moral
History of the Indies* that the first people to live in the New World may
have come from Asia, following the migratory animals whom they
hunted. Acosta's brilliant intuition—made with no knowledge of the
existence of the narrow Bering Straits, or of the Ice Age that created the
Bering land bridge between Asia and America—was later substantiated
by scientific research.

Today, most scholars accept both the geological evidence about the
Bering land bridge and recent DNA research that indicates that North
American Indians and certain Asians come from a common stock. It
should, however, be recognized that many Indians themselves are suspicious of these theories, and firmly believe that they have "always" lived
in North America.

As yet, research has not established when the first small bands of
animals and people (known as Paleo-Indians) began to cross from
Asia into America, although some scholars have suggested that migration may have begun as long as 40,000 years ago. Probably sometime
between about 20,000 to 12,000 years ago, as the great ice cap and
glaciers slowly began to recede, it became possible for increasing numbers of people to move deeper and deeper into the North American
continent.

These pictographs found on a rock shelter near Adamana, Arizona, are typical of many carved or painted in caves or rock shelters in the South-west. They provide evidence of the prehistoric settlements of Indians in North America. *(National Archives)*

The melting ice became the rivers, streams, and lakes that irrigated the plains, creating the extensive grasslands that gradually spread across some 750,000 square miles in the heart of the continent. This period of rich pasturage was followed by an arid cycle, during which many of the largest animals, such as the giant sloths and mastodons, and many smaller species, died out. The lack of human remains from this period on the plains has led many archaeologists to think that most of the Indians left the harsh stretches of the Great Plains and settled in the Southwest and the eastern woodlands at about this time.

Archaeological remains suggest that Indians began to move back into the Great Plains in considerable numbers around the 13th century, again hunting migratory animals, especially the great buffalo herds that were moving up into the plains from Mexico at this time. Many Indians, usually called the nomadic Indians, lived as hunters and gatherers, following the herds over the plains. Others (known as the sedentary Indians) lived for all or most of the year in round or oblong earthen dwellings and cultivated corn, squash, and beans. Often these sedentary Indians left their villages in the summer to hunt buffalo, returning home when they had ample supplies of preserved meat (pemmican) for the winter.

The Plains Indians devised a rich and complex mythology that attempted to answer questions about their origins and early life. However, as with any mythological system, these myths are best understood as attempts to comprehend the unknown, rather than as a reliable folk memory of the past. For this reason, it becomes easier to get a sense of life on the plains when the Europeans arrive and begin to write accounts of what they saw, even though these accounts have to be regarded with caution, as they often contain misunderstandings and error. The first Europeans to explore the Great Plains were some 200 Spanish soldiers led up into the plains in 1541 by the explorer Francisco Vásquez de Coronado. Coronado had already been disappointed in his search for the Seven Cities of Cibola in New Mexico, rumored to contain fabulous wealth, but which were in fact only a group of pueblo villages.

While in New Mexico, Coronado met a Pawnee Indian whose turbanlike headdress earned him the nickname of the Turk. The Turk told Coronado that the wealth he sought lay east of Cibola, at Quivera, in what is now Kansas. But like Cibola, Quivera proved to be a simple village. In disgust, Coronado killed the Turk and began the long trek back to Mexico, where he dismissed the land his expedition had visited as a vast desert, a "sea of grass" inhabited only by scattered Indians and vast herds of buffalo. In a report to the king of Spain, Coronado wrote that it was impossible to number the buffalo, "for while I was journeying through the plains, there was not a day that I lost sight of them."

Coronado was right about the abundance of buffalo. Estimates of their number at this time range from 15 million to 50 million. But Coronado's impression that the Great Plains was a desert, suitable only for Indians and buffalo, was anything but accurate. Coronado had no way of knowing that what seemed an endless journey to him—830 miles from Mexico to Quivera and then 520 miles back on a more direct route—barely touched on the Great Plains, or that he saw only one or two of the many tribes living there.

The 98th meridian, which cuts through the Dakotas, Nebraska, Kansas, Oklahoma, and Texas, splits the Great Plains into two contrasting geographical areas. The land between the 98th meridian and the Mississippi is more prairie than plain. Here broad rivers and good rainfall created a land of dense woodlands and potentially rich farmland hidden beneath stretches of grass six feet and more in height. The Indians here at the time of the 19th-century Plains Indian Wars included the Hidatsa, Mandan, Pawnee, Osage, and Omaha, who lived in settled communities and farmed.

The part of the Great Plains that earned it the reputation of an inhospitable desert lay west of the 98th meridian. Here rainfall was infrequent, the soil was poor, and mile upon mile was covered with the short grass called buffalo grass. By the time of the Plains Indian Wars, this was home to the Comanche, Cheyenne, Blackfeet, Crow, and Sioux

INTRODUCTION OF THE HORSE INTO NORTH AMERICA

Note: Lines and arrows indicate approximate diffusion routes of horse-related culture out of Mexico to Indian tribes; dates indicate approximate years horses reached the various areas (with modern boundaries).

SPANISH INTRODUCE HORSE INTO MEXICO IN 1518

N

0   400 miles
0   400 km

© 2000 Carl Waldman and Facts On File, Inc.

(the Lakota, Nakota, and Dakota). This was the land where, in the words of the cowboy song "Home on the Range," the buffalo roamed and the deer and the antelope played. This was a place of frigid winters and scorching summers, of sudden, unpredictable changes in the weather, so that a hot summer day could be interrupted by a hailstorm, or a deadly tornado could whirl out of a clear blue sky. While Coronado found nothing of value among the Indians, the Indians soon realized that the Spaniards had something of immense value to them: the horse, which they called the "giant dog" or the "mystery dog." Horses do not seem to have arrived on the Great Plains in numbers great enough to change Indian life until the late 17th century. In 1680, the Pueblo Indians of New Mexico rose against the Spanish, who abandoned their settlements, leaving behind many horses. These horses may have been among the first to be taken over by local Indians, who in turn traded them to other tribes.

The culture which most people associate with the Plains Indians—the nomadic culture dependent on horses and buffalo—only developed fully in the century before the Plains Indian Wars. Almost half the Plains Indians were members of the Sioux, the group most closely associated in the popular imagination with the Great Plains—but, in fact, one of the last groups to arrive there. "Sioux" was not the name they used for themselves; they used Dakota, Lakota, or Nakota, each of which had subgroups. The Teton Lakota, for instance, included: Mini Conjon, Oohenonpa, the Oglala, Brute, Hunkpapa, Itazipco, and Sihasapa. In the late 17th century, missionaries encountered Sioux in Minnesota (these would be the Santee Dakota Sioux), but by the mid-18th century, most had been pushed out of that area by the Iroquois and had joined the Plains Indians. By the mid-19th century, the Sioux made up one of the two most powerful groups on the Great Plains. The other, of course, was composed of whites of European descent.

Travelers such as George Catlin marveled at the diversity of every aspect of life among the Plains Indians, whose many tribes spoke six distinct languages and had enough dialects to make sign language a necessity for communication. In his *Illustrations of the Manners, Customs, and Condition of the North American Indian*, published in 1857, Catlin stated that he had devoted himself to painting and documenting the differences in the "living manners, customs, and character" of the Indians. Catlin's sketches and paintings, along with those of his contemporary Karl Bodmer, document the enormous differences in daily

The Original Mobile Home
THE TIPI

AT THE TIME OF THE PLAINS INDIANS WARS, SOME tribes on the Great Plains, including the Hidatsa, Mandan, Pawnee, and Omaha, lived most of the year in earthen dwellings, subsisting off the crops they raised. Still, the majority of the Plains Indians were migratory peoples who followed the vast buffalo herds across the plains. The buffalo was their primary source of food (the meat), clothing (the hides and fur), weapons and needles (the bones), containers (the bladder and stomach), ornaments (the tail), and toys (the horns). Perhaps most important, the buffalo was the source of the Plains Indians' usual dwelling place: the tipi. When a family needed a tipi, women in the tribe cured the hides and stitched them together. Men shaped the poles that would support the conical tipi. The tipi had as its greatest advantage that it was lightweight and portable. European Americans who spent time in Indian tipis often complained about the congestion, smells, and smoke, but Elaine Goodale Eastman, who was a teacher on the Great Sioux Reservation in the 1880s and 1890s, thought it an ideal dwelling. "The chimney flaps, properly regulated, carry off most of the smoke," she wrote, "and the whole is easily transformed in a few minutes into a breezy awning for summer weather." By the time Eastman left the Great Sioux Reservation, Indians were forbidden to live in tipis: The federal government feared that if the Indians could strike camp and move about easily, they would be too hard to control.

life of the Plains Indians, from Mandan living in their earthen lodge villages to Crow living in tipis that Catlin described as "white as linen."

Despite the great diversity in almost every aspect of daily life among the Native Americans of the plains, it is possible to identify a number of common elements in their life on the eve of the Plains Indian Wars. Among these shared elements, the importance of the horse and the buffalo and what has been called "the great war game" are especially important.

It is impossible to overestimate the extent to which the horse changed Plains Indian life. On foot, a single hunter could, at best, hope to pick off a single stray or sickly buffalo from the herd. On horseback,

THE GREAT PLAINS AND ITS PEOPLE

one man could run down a number of buffalo with relative ease. Consequently, even when a tribe had only a few horses, its meat supply was enormously increased. Before the coming of the horse, when a tribe moved, it did so on foot, with dogs pulling the wooden A-shaped travois that held family possessions, including the buffalo-skin tipis and support poles. Since a dog could pull only about 60 pounds, tipis had to be relatively small. A horse could easily pull some 250 pounds and much longer support poles. This meant that tipis could be larger and infinitely more comfortable. Once dogs were not needed for transport, they became a food source, with young puppies being esteemed as a particular delicacy.

If the horse was the critical means of transport for the Plains Indians, the buffalo was the primary source of virtually all the necessities of life. Just as the Navajo thought of the sheep (also acquired from the Spanish) as their mother and father because they supplied both food and clothing, so the Plains Indians regarded the buffalo as a sacred source of virtually all they required.

Before any hunt, the religious leaders (sometimes called medicine men) would offer prayers of apology for killing the buffalo and prayers

This Cheyenne family is shown with its horse hitched to a travois, the French-Canadian name given to the rack on which the Plains Indians lashed their tipi and other possessions to move them about.
(National Archives)

Buffalo meat can be seen drying in this Arapaho camp near Fort Dodge, Kansas, 1870. *(National Archives)*

of thanks that the buffalo was willing to die. Different tribes had count-less legends about the buffalo, with the Lakota, for example, believing that they lived in a giant cave under the earth. If a buffalo was properly honored when it was killed, another would spring forth from the cave to replace it. Not only was buffalo meat a dietary staple, but buffalo hides were used to make tipis, small boats, drinking cups and storage vessels, blankets, moccasins, and clothing. Tribal records, pictographs showing great battles and other events, were painted on buffalo hides. Buffalo bones were fashioned into needles and honed into blades, the large shoulder bones of the buffalo were fashioned into hoes and plows, and buffalo sinews became threads and bow strings.

Both the nomadic and sedentary Plains Indians tended to live for most of the year in small bands, or villages, and the entire tribe came together only occasionally. In the 19th century some 1,600 nomadic Kiowa lived and hunted in 10 to 20 bands, while the sedentary Mandan at their most powerful farmed in 13 villages. In addition to belonging to the larger tribe, and a particular band, Indians belonged to a num-ber of other groups, from the individual birth family and kinship clans to clans for different age and interest groups not unlike today's sports and recreational clubs.

THE GREAT PLAINS AND ITS PEOPLE

Men and women had clearly defined roles in Plains Indians society. Women were responsible for child rearing, farming, cooking, and making pemmican and clothing. The men were the warriors, hunters, and political and religious leaders. Training began early: little girls practiced sewing buffalo-skin garments while little boys on ponies practiced hunting buffalo by running down buffalo calves. Boys usually took their place among the warriors in their teens and married shortly thereafter. It was not unusual for a wealthy man to have several wives, an arrangement that allowed the women to share chores, especially the heavy work of breaking camp. An Omaha Native American explained the custom this way: "I must take another wife. My old wife is not strong enough now to do all her work alone."

Since there was no such thing as individual land ownership, wealth was defined in horses and goods such as buffalo robes or guns and clothing acquired from white traders. A wealthy man was held in high esteem, but the aspect of wealth that was most admired was generosity: At great feasts and funerals, a wealthy Indian might give away virtually all his possessions—and then begin again to accumulate wealth. In consequence, Plains Indian tribes frequently launched armed raids to gain horses—or to gain revenge against a tribe that had raided the all-important horse supply.

This painting (by John M. Stanley, ca. 1854) of Blackfoot Indians chasing buffalo in Montana confirms that the culture of the Plains Indians depended on both the horse and the buffalo. *(National Archives)*

PLAINS INDIAN WARS

These Paiute children in northern Arizona are playing a game called wolf-and-deer, clearly designed to teach them the ways of the animals with whom they lived and on whom their own lives depended. By the late 19th century, "reformers" would try to obliterate all such traces of "savage" culture. *(National Archives)*

Warfare was of supreme importance for the Plains Indians, and, except for religious leaders, a man's position in his tribe almost invariably reflected his bravery as a warrior. The vast extent of the Great Plains meant that wars to win territory were relatively infrequent. Since the point of combat was seldom to destroy another tribe and take over its land, combat became a highly stylized ritual (the great war game) in which acts of individual bravery were of paramount importance. Returning home with a string of horses and a record of coups, the touching of a living foe, was far more important than killing and scalping an enemy. In fact, among the Plains Indians, only the Cree and the Teton put a high value on gathering scalps. To this day, scholars debate whether the Europeans first introduced scalping to the Indians or the Indians introduced it to the first Europeans.

Like most Native Americans, the people of the plains believed in a creator, sometimes called the Great Spirit. Almost all believed that a person's soul, or spirit, survived death, and many believed that the after-life was an ideal version of life on earth: sunny skies, reunion with loved ones, and an endless supply of buffalo.

Virtually every aspect of Plains Indian life was permeated by religious beliefs and ceremonies. Every individual household, and every tribe, had a medicine bundle containing sacred amulets, such as feathers and stones, whose power was called upon before any important undertaking. Every buffalo hunt was preceded by prayers and dances to woo the prey, and followed by prayers and dances of thanksgiving. No raid took place before the religious leaders of the tribe consulted the spirits and omens to see if the outcome would be favorable.

By and large, the most important religious ceremonies were open only to men; furthermore, in some tribes only men could be religious

The Role of Medicine Men and Women

MEDICINE MEN AND WOMEN WERE IMPORTANT AND powerful figures among the Plains Indians. Any young man could decide to become a medicine man (sometimes called a shaman), although some families had a tradition of producing numerous medicine men. After several years of study with older medicine men, the candidate usually withdrew from society for a period of intense meditation. During this time, he hoped for a vision that would tell him what animal—perhaps the bear, elk, or eagle—would be his protector and symbol. At the end of the candidate's period of meditation, the older medicine men in the tribe welcomed him ceremonially into their company. Medicine women were often the daughters and wives of medicine men, but sometimes were women whose special powers were recognized within the tribe. Medicine men performed important rituals, especially before hunts and battles. In most tribes, they were also responsible for rituals to ensure good crops and successful harvest. Medicine women were particularly gifted in curing diseases, foreseeing the future, and influencing the weather. Both medicine men and women were thought to possess powers of interpreting omens and portents and communicating with the spirits of the departed.

A Navajo Indian dance, Old Fort Defiance, New Mexico, 1873
(National Archives)

leaders, known as shamans or medicine men. The Sun Dance was of central significance among a number of tribes, including the Pawnee, Wichita, Omaha, and Dakota, Lakota, and Nakota Sioux. Usually the Sun Dance was held at a time when the entire tribe was assembled and one or more men sought a vision. The vision seeker would fast and dance for several days, staring up into the sun, until he received a vision. Sometimes, the vision seeker would mutilate his body, cutting out small strips of flesh as sacrificial offerings to the spirits as he danced, as the Hunkpapa Lakota Sioux chief Sitting Bull was to do shortly before the Battle of the Little Bighorn.

Another important religious ritual shared by many Plains Indians tribes was a purification ceremony, often done as a coming-of-age ceremony, which took place in a special building, the sweat lodge. Like the grueling Sun Dance, the sweat ceremony—which alternated sessions in the fiery hot sweat lodge with plunges into cold water—was thought to purify the soul and prepare the participant for a vision. Indians often took their adult names from messages received in these visions, which also frequently revealed what talismans an individual should wear, and what the outcome of an upcoming battle would be.

Of the series of government forts and private trading posts across the West, perhaps the best known was Old Bent's Fort, set up in 1832 in southeastern Colorado by three traders, Ceran St. Vrain and the brothers William and Charles Bent. *(Library of Congress)*

The sweat lodge was also sometimes used to treat the aches and pains of daily life—a habit that was to have deadly consequences when non-Indian visitors introduced the smallpox virus to the plains. A devastating series of smallpox epidemics swept the plains between 1780 and the last great epidemic, which began in 1837 when smallpox carried by a passenger on a Missouri steamboat rapidly spread among the Plains Indians. Medical historians estimate that reliance on the sweat house to "sweat out" the smallpox fever may have doubled Indian fatalities.

The Mandan were the most seriously affected by the smallpox epidemic of 1837. These were the people whose dignity and beauty so impressed George Catlin when he visited their settlements near Fort Clark on the Missouri in 1832 that he concluded that they could not possibly really be Indians. Even though he devoted his life to documenting Indian life, Catlin shared his society's deep prejudices, and finally concluded that the Mandan must "have sprung from some other origin than that of other North American Indians." Of the 1,600 Mandan whom Catlin visited in 1832, only about 200 survived the epidemic. As for the other Plains Indians, smallpox left them seriously weakened, only years before they had to face their greatest challenge: the hostilities known as the Plains Indian Wars.

4

WAR ON THE
SOUTHERN PLAINS

Although the Dakota, Lakota, and Nakota Sioux were the largest and strongest tribes living on the Great Plains, in the 19th century, they were by no means the only group to fight in the Plains Indian Wars. Four other important nomadic buffalo-hunting tribes—the Arapaho, Cheyenne, Comanche, and Kiowa—repeatedly clashed, first with other Indian tribes and then with white settlers and soldiers on the southern plains. The most important engagements took place during two series of skirmishes that, despite the lack of a clear beginning or end, are usually considered to be conflicts distinct enough to be called wars: the Cheyenne and Arapaho War of 1864–65, fought when most of the United States was focused on the Civil War, and the Red River War of 1874–75, which effectively put an end to the wars on the southern plains.

Like the Sioux, the Arapaho and the more powerful Cheyenne seem to have entered the plains from Minnesota in the 17th and 18th centuries. By the mid-19th century, the Cheyenne and Arapaho, both originally members of the Algonquian language group of tribes, had split into northern and southern groups. The Northern Arapaho and Cheyenne lived east of the Rocky Mountains in Wyoming, and the Southern Arapaho and Cheyenne lived near Fort Bent on the Arkansas River in Colorado. Both the Southern Cheyenne and the Southern Arapaho had been persuaded to settle near Fort Bent in 1835 by Indian traders William and Charlie Bent, who realized that the Indians could supply them with buffalo robes.

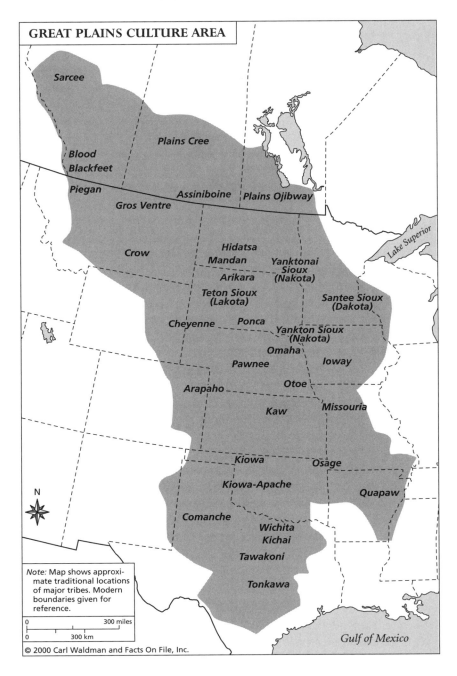

GREAT PLAINS CULTURE AREA

Sarcee

Plains Cree

Blood
Blackfeet

Piegan

Gros Ventre

Assiniboine

Plains Ojibway

Lake Superior

Crow

Hidatsa
Mandan

Yanktonai
Sioux
(Nakota)

Arikara

Teton Sioux
(Lakota)

Santee Sioux
(Dakota)

Cheyenne

Ponca

Yankton Sioux
(Nakota)

Omaha

Pawnee

Ioway

Arapaho

Otoe

Kaw

Missouria

Kiowa

Osage

Kiowa-Apache

Quapaw

Comanche

Wichita
Kichai

Tawakoni

Tonkawa

N

Note: Map shows approximate traditional locations of major tribes. Modern boundaries given for reference.

| 0 | | 300 miles |
| 0 | 300 km | |

© 2000 Carl Waldman and Facts On File, Inc.

Gulf of Mexico

Just as the Arapahos allied themselves with the more powerful Cheyenne, the Kiowa linked themselves with the mighty Comanche. Between the 17th and 19th centuries, the Kiowa moved south from the area of the Upper Missouri River, ultimately settling in Oklahoma, Texas, New Mexico, and Kansas. The Comanche, who were superb riders and warriors, had migrated from western Wyoming south to the southern plains, which they dominated. Both the Kiowa and the Comanche ranged as far south as Mexico, where they often raided settlements for horses.

By the 1800s, the Arapaho, Cheyenne, Kiowa, and Comanche were among the most powerful tribes living on the plains. By the early 1840s, the U.S. government had resettled some 90,000 eastern Indians among the 250,000 Indians already living on the plains. At midcentury, most of these newcomers lived in the Indian Territory, which contained most of present-day Oklahoma and parts of Kansas. One of the many problems that the government in Washington had not anticipated when it settled eastern Indians west of the Mississippi was that the Indians already living on the plains would not be at all pleased at this influx of strangers into their hunting grounds.

In 1854, the Kiowa and Comanche, along with a number of Arapaho and Cheyenne, set upon several tribes of resettled Sac and Fox and Potawatomi Indians in Kansas. The skirmish was inconclusive and, before long, the established plains tribes focused their attention on a far greater threat than Indian newcomers: the whites, who were moving across the plains in greater and greater numbers.

These early settlers traveled west along a network of trails. In 1822, the Santa Fe Trail between Independence, Missouri, and Santa Fe, New Mexico, had opened; in 1842, the first wagons had moved across the Oregon Trail from points along the Missouri west to Oregon; in 1847 the Mormons began their westward migration along the Mormon Trail, which branched off the Oregon Trail to Utah; and, in 1849, the gold seekers followed the Oregon Trail west to the Snake River in the Oregon Territory before heading south across Utah to California.

The Plains Indians did what they could to stop traffic on the trails that ran through the heart of their hunting territory by attacking wagon trains whenever possible. It was these attacks that led to the meeting at Fort Laramie in southeast Wyoming in 1851, and the treaty discussed earlier.

Like virtually every other agreement signed by the Indians and the whites, the Fort Laramie treaty soon ran into trouble, as did a similar

This 19th-century engraving presents an undeniable fact: Immigrant trains were sometimes attacked by Indians. But the Indians felt this was the only way to stop the loss of their lands. *(Library of Congress)*

treaty signed later the same year at Fort Atkinson, Kansas, by the United States, the Kiowa, and the Comanche. The U.S. government dragged its heels about distributing the Indians' annuity and the Indians continued to live where they chose and to raid isolated parties of settlers moving west along the trails.

In 1858, gold was discovered at Pikes Peak in the Rocky Mountains of Colorado, and prospectors headed west along the Smoky Hill Trail that ran between the Platte and the Arkansas Rivers, cutting across some of the best buffalo hunting grounds. In 1859, 100,000 prospectors followed the new trail west, totally disrupting the buffalo hunting season. In addition, many of the prospectors who did not find gold stayed in the area and attempted to homestead and farm Indian land. By 1863, government agents were reporting to Washington that malnutrition was widespread among the Cheyenne and Arapaho.

Given the Indians' widespread hunger, it was not surprising that there should be an increasing number of run-ins between whites and Indians. One incident is believed to have sparked the Cheyenne and Arapaho War of 1864–65. On April 11, 1864, a Colorado rancher named Ripley galloped to Fort Sanborn, near Denver, and reported that a band of Cheyenne Indians had rustled (stolen) some of his livestock. As in the 1854 Fort Laramie incident, a detachment was sent out from the fort to find the rustlers and, once again, when the soldiers found the Indians, things soon went wrong. The Cheyenne were prepared to surrender the horses (which they said were strays), but not their weapons. As the soldiers attempted to disarm the band, fighting broke out; when it was over, several soldiers and an unknown number of Indians were dead.

As soon as the news got back to Fort Sanborn, the consensus among the army officers was that the Cheyenne were on the warpath and had to be stopped. Indian trader William Bent, who had a Cheyenne wife and three children, tried in vain to maintain peaceful relations with both sides,

Gold and Other Rushes

IN 1848, WHILE BUILDING A SAWMILL FOR SWISS immigrant John Sutter, a carpenter James Marshall found gold nuggets in a stream near Sacramento, California. When news of the discovery reached the East, it sparked the gold rush of 1849. As many as 40,000 prospectors headed west. Although everyone hoped to get rich quick, few did, and many lost what money they had. Sutter himself was one of the first casualties of the gold rush: His herds of cattle were killed by hungry prospectors, and the bankrupt Sutter fled to Pennsylvania. When gold was discovered 10 years later at Pikes Peak in Colorado's Rocky Mountains, there was yet another westward stampede. When the gold ran out, many of the prospectors turned to homesteading, hastening the end of hunting for buffalo on the Great Plains. It was gold that brought the prospectors west, but it was the land that kept them there and turned them into settlers. This provoked the greatest rush of all: the 19th and early 20th century rush to get cheap farm and ranch land away from the Plains Indians. Legislation paved the way for the land rush. Under the terms of the Homesteading Act of 1862 and the General Allotment Act of 1887 (often called the Dawes Act) a vast amount of land west of the Mississippi was opened to settlement. By the turn of the 20th century, almost 500,000 new homesteaders had filed land claims in Kansas, Nebraska, and the Dakotas. Probably the best-known land rush was one of the last: In 1889, settlers streamed into the new state of Oklahoma (which had previously been set aside for Indians). So many jumped the gun, racing off before the land was officially open for homesteaders, that they gave the new state its nickname: the "Sooner" state.

but the Cheyenne and Arapaho continued to attack isolated settlements. In June, a band of Arapaho killed and mutilated two settlers and their infant daughter on a farm just 20 miles from Denver. When the three bodies were exhibited in Denver, residents panicked. Governor John Evans pleaded with Washington to send home one of Colorado's two regiments then fighting in the Civil War. "Large bodies of Indians," Evans informed Washington, "are undoubtedly near to Denver, and we are in danger of destruction both from attacks of Indians and from starvation."

When Washington informed Evans that the Colorado troops were needed to fight Confederates, Evans realized that he would have to deal with the Cheyenne and Arapaho himself. Evans swiftly authorized creation of a third Colorado regiment of volunteers who would serve for 100 days—enough time, Evans thought, to settle matters with the Cheyenne and their allies. Evans ordered the "Hundred Dazers," as they were known, to "kill and destroy" all "hostile Indians." But before the regiment could move, Indian agent William Bent tried again to convince the Cheyenne and Arapaho, the Comanche and the Kiowa, to meet with Governor Evans and make peace.

On September 28, a great number of Cheyenne and Arapaho met with Governor Evans and Col. John Chivington, commander of the new Colorado regiment, at Camp Weld, just outside Denver. The Indians

Established in 1849 as a military outpost along the Oregon Trail, Fort Laramie, Wyoming, was the site of the 1851 treaty intended to protect land belonging to the Plains Indians. *(Library of Congress, Prints & Photographs Division [LC-D4-13794])*

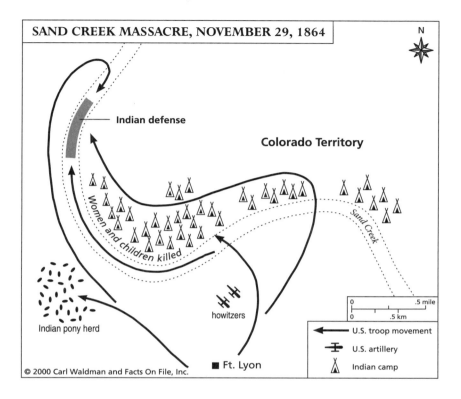

SAND CREEK MASSACRE, NOVEMBER 29, 1864

N

Indian defense

Colorado Territory

Women and children killed

Sand Creek

Indian pony herd

howitzers

0 .5 mile
0 .5 km

U.S. troop movement
U.S. artillery
Indian camp

Ft. Lyon

© 2000 Carl Waldman and Facts On File, Inc.

agreed to cease from hostilities, and camped outside nearby Fort Lyon, where they stayed until November. Then, Major Wynkoop, commander of Fort Weld, gave the Indians assurances of peace and told them to move to a new camp, some 40 miles away at Sand Creek. There matters might have rested had it not been for Colonel Chivington, who arrived at Fort Lyon on November 28 with some 1,000 of the the "Hundred Dazers."

Chivington proceeded to take matters into his own hands in a way that seems incomprehensible: Over the protests of several of the soldiers already at Fort Lyon, who pointed out that the Indians were settled peacefully at Sand Creek, Chivington led his men on a night march, arriving at Sand Creek at dawn.

Urging his soldiers to "Kill and scalp all; nits make lice," Chivington attacked the Cheyenne and Arapaho encampment of some 200 men and 500 women and children in the Big South Bend of the Sand Creek.

When Chief Black Kettle saw the soldiers coming, he reassured his people that they had nothing to fear, and raised both the U.S. flag and a white flag to remind the approaching soldiers that the Indians were at peace. As Black Kettle raised the two flags, the Third Colorado Cavalry opened fire, wounding the chief in the hip. Nearby, Chief White Antelope had just begun his death song—"Nothing lives long, except the earth and mountains"—when he was shot.

Chivington's men took his orders to kill and scalp to heart: the fight lasted some four hours and about 163 Cheyenne were killed, including 110 women and children. The Third Colorado Cavalry lost nine men. When it was over, Chivington sent word to Denver that he had destroyed a Cheyenne village of from "nine hundred to a thousand warriors." As to the Hundred Dazers, Chivington reported that "all did nobly," a sentiment echoed by the *Denver News,* which reported Sand Creek as a "great victory." Proof of the victory came when the 100 scalps taken at Sand Creek were displayed on stage during the intermission of a Denver stage show.

Despite the public acclaim for Chivington, some of his own soldiers publicly questioned whether Sand Creek had been a glorious victory or a shameful massacre. When asked what he thought of Chivington, the famous Indian scout Kit Carson replied that he was a coward. Both military and congressional investigations held the year after Sand Creek condemned Chivington's actions, but as he had left the military, he could not be court-martialed or punished.

In the following months, infuriated by what had happened at Sand Creek, the Sioux, Cheyenne and Arapaho, Kiowa, and Comanche banded together and attacked wherever they could from the northern plains deep into Texas, pursued by Brig. Gen. Patrick Connor and 700 soldiers. Connor could not defeat the Indians, and the Indians could not rid the plains of the whites.

When the Confederacy surrendered in 1865, ending the Civil War, the regular army soldiers who were not discharged were free to take on the Plains Indians. Gen. William Tecumseh Sherman was placed in command of the Division of the Mississippi, a military district that included all the land between the Rockies and the Mississippi, from the Canadian border in the north to Texas in the south. Sherman was in no doubt about his mission: "We have now selected and provided reservations for all," he said. "All who cling to their old hunting grounds are hostile and will remain so till killed off."

After the Civil War,
Gen. William T.
Sherman went on
to command troops
in the West.
(National Archives)

In 1867, Gen. Winfield Hancock, Commander of the Department of the Missouri, pursued the Sioux and Cheyenne across much of Kansas, Colorado, and Nebraska. "Pursued" is the critical word. Hancock's six infantry companies almost never caught up with the Indians, despite the best efforts of the hell-for-leather field commander George Armstrong Custer, acting commander of the Seventh Cavalry. Nor did the Medicine Lodge Treaty of 1867, in which the usual promises were exchanged, put an end to the fighting. Although most of the Cheyenne, Kiowa, Comanche, and Arapaho agreed when they met at Medicine Lodge Creek in southern Kansas to settle on reservations in Oklahoma and Kansas, many refused to move there. Still others moved to the reservations, but could not stand to remain and soon left. Consequently, hostilities between Indians and whites continued.

In 1868 Black Kettle, who had survived Sand Creek, led many of the Cheyenne and Arapaho off the reservation into the more agreeable Washita Valley in western Oklahoma, thus violating the Medicine Lodge Treaty of 1867. When Black Kettle notified the reservation authorities that he had left, he got word to return at once. He was making preparations to do this when George Custer and the Seventh Cavalry arrived.

On November 27, 1868—almost four years to the day from the Sand Creek massacre—Custer's Seventh Cavalry, with the regimental band playing "Gerry Owen" and "The Girl I Left Behind Me," attacked and killed Black Kettle and most of his tribe in the Battle of the Washita. As at Sand Creek, what some saw as a military victory others saw as simple massacre. Editorials in *The New York Times* criticized Custer's assault on a seemingly peaceable tribe. Whatever public opinion might say "back east," increasingly, no distinction would be made on the plains between "hostile" and "friendly" Indians. This philosophy was best summed up in Gen. Philip Sheridan' remark that "The only good Indians I ever saw were dead," which passed into popular legend as the phrase "The only good Indian is a dead Indian."

Since his arrival on the plains at the end of the Civil War, Sheridan, now the commander of the Division of the Missouri, had engaged in a sweeping offensive against the Southern Cheyenne, who retaliated by attacking small settlements in Kansas. Most of these encounters between the Indians and soldiers were hit-and-run affairs, and many took place in the Dakota Territory near Fort Phil Kearny, which the

This print from a wood engraving shows prisoners from Black Kettle's camp captured by General Custer traveling through the snow.
(Library of Congress, Prints & Photographs Division [LC-USZ62-117248])

Plains Indians and Their Dogs and Horses

WHEN CHRISTOPHER COLUMBUS ARRIVED IN THE New World, the Indians had only one domesticated animal—the dog (which the first arrivals in North America had most likely brought with them from Asia). Dogs (especially puppies) were valued for their meat; adult dogs were trained to assist in hunting. Before the arrival of European settlers most Indian groups did not use wheels for transportation, and dogs were the Indian's only beast of burden, dragging loads behind them on the A-shaped wooden carrier known as the travois. However useful dogs were, their importance was rapidly eclipsed when Spanish explorers introduced the horse onto the Great Plains. At first, the Indians thought of the horse simply as a very large dog, often calling horses "sacred dogs." Most Indians never acquired a taste for horseflesh, but immediately saw the possibilities that the horse could bring to life on the plains. Most important, the horse meant that the Plains Indians could be mobile in a way that they had never been before. Hunting buffalo from horseback allowed for much greater success, hence greater prosperity for the tribe. Warfare from horseback allowed for wider ranging raids. Even domestic architecture was affected: Before the coming of the horse to the Great Plains, dogs pulled the tipis behind them on the travois. Horses could pull a heavier and longer travois, thus tipis could be made much larger and more comfortable. Almost immediately, horses were the accepted standard by which a family or a tribe's wealth was measured. Young men set off on raids simply to acquire horses, just one of the ways that the coming of the horse profoundly changed life on the Great Plains. Indeed, the Blackfeet Indians to this day refer to their "dog days" as the time before the horse came to the Great Plains.

Indians called "the hated fort on the Piney." In the Wagon Box Fight on August 2, 1867, Capt. James W. Powell had hardly time to shout "Men, here they come! Take your places and shoot to kill" when a band of Lakota led by Oglalu Lakota Chief Red Cloud swept out of the hills and attacked his soldiers, who were gathering firewood in a stand of trees about six miles west of the fort. A trapper who fought alongside the soldiers later recalled that he "kept eight guns pretty well het up for mor'n three hours." Thanks to their superior firepower, Powell's men drove the Indians away, inflicting such heavy casualties that they later called the skirmish "Medicine Fight," in recognition of the soldiers' "good medicine" that day.

In the winter of 1867, General Sheridan mounted a major campaign by leading the three-pronged attack against the Cheyenne in New Mexico, Colorado, and Kansas, in which Custer leveled Black Kettle's village. Nonetheless, fighting on the southern plains continued off and on until March of 1869, when Custer managed to secure the surrender of most of the Southern Cheyenne and Arapaho whom he had trapped near the Sweetwater Creek on the Staked Plain of the Texas Panhandle. Custer took three chiefs as hostages to guarantee that the Indians would return to their North Texas reservation, which they did that spring. This effectively put an end to the freedom of the Southern Cheyenne and Arapaho.

The final great conflict on the southern plains, the Red River War (sometimes called the Buffalo War) of 1874–75, primarily involved the

The coming of the railroads to the plains after the Civil War intensified the slaughter of the buffalo, making it even more "necessary"—and easier—to kill the animals that stood in the way of "progress."
(Library of Congress)

Comanche and Kiowa of Texas. From about 1840 until the outbreak of the Red River War, the Texas Rangers had tried repeatedly to subdue the Comanche. In 1864, Col. Kit Carson had managed to burn much of the Comanche winter supplies, but was unable to obtain their surrender. Nor did the seven forts built along the Red River as far south as the Rio Grande really undermine Comanche power.

In May of 1874, considerable numbers of Comanche, Kiowa, Cheyenne, and Arapaho left their reservations in Indian Territory (Oklahoma) for the Texas Panhandle, where they camped together and held a three-day Sun Dance. The Indians seem to have had two things in mind when they left the reservations: first, to resume their traditional nomadic way of life, and secondly, to attack the white buffalo hunters who were decimating the buffalo herds.

The development of improved methods of tanning and softening buffalo hides in the 1870s soon made buffalo skins as desirable as cowhide—and a lot cheaper. Buffalo hunters, accompanied by the "hide men" who skinned the animals and the traders who bought and sold the hides, flooded the plains, shooting, skinning, and buying up literally millions of skins. One hunter, Orlando Bond, claimed to have killed 5,855 buffalo in a two-month period. As buffalo became scarce, the white hunters increasingly infiltrated the Indian hunting grounds south of the Arkansas River, ignoring a prohibition in the Medicine Lodge Treaty. The Indians realized that they had to stop the booming buffalo skin trade if they were going to have any buffalo left to hunt themselves.

Although the different southern plains Indians had common goals, they might never have united had it not been for the teachings of Isatai (also spelled Eeshatai), a Comanche medicine man who preached that the Great Spirit had revealed to him a special yellow body paint that would halt bullets. On June 27, 1874, persuaded of their invulnerability by Isatai, several hundred Comanche and an unknown number of Kiowa, Cheyenne, and Arapaho warriors mounted an attack on the hated trading post of Adobe Walls, in the Texas Panhandle, where buffalo hunters came to sell hides to traders. The Cheyenne war chief was Quanah Parker, the son of a Cheyenne chief and Hannah Parker, a white woman kidnapped by the Cheyenne as a young girl.

Despite Isatai's promises, the Indians were not invulnerable to the bullets from the heavy buffalo guns fired by the 28 buffalo hunters and traders inside the trading post. After their initial attack was rebuffed, the Indians laid siege to Adobe Walls, but one of those inside slipped out and rode to Dodge City for aid. Reinforcements arrived in early July and helped to evacuate Adobe Walls, which the Indians promptly burned. With Isatai totally discredited, the various tribes separated and scattered across Texas, New Mexico, Colorado, and Kansas, attacking isolated settlements whenever possible.

General Sheridan reacted angrily to news of the burning of Adobe Walls and the subsequent Indian attacks and sent off virtually all his available troops—some 5,000 in all—in pursuit. In September, Col. Ranald Mackenzie, who was leading the 450 men of the Fourth Cavalry, got word that a sizable number of Cheyenne, Comanche, and Kiowa led by Quanah Parker had set up their winter camp deep in the 120-mile-long Palo Duro Canyon on the Red River in northwest Texas. Despite his numbers, Mackenzie managed a surprise attack down a steep trail that led to the canyon. Years later, Capt. Robert G. Carter, who rode with Mackenzie, described him as a "poor rider" due to "his failing to take care of himself and his three wounds received during the Civil War, plus

Among many testimonies to the extent of the mass destruction of the buffalo is this picture of some 40,000 buffalo hides in a Kansas dealer's yard in 1878, waiting to be processed and sent east. *(National Archives)*

Quanah Parker, a
Kwahadi Comanche
chief, led a group of
Comanche, Cheyenne,
and Kiowa in the
Palo Duro battle.
(National Archives)

a bad arrow wound in his thigh in the 1871 campaign." Still, Carter reported, in combat "Mackenzie hung on like a bulldog until the Indians begged him to let go." At Palo Duro, when Mackenzie attacked, the Indians fled deeper into the canyon, losing only five warriors.

Despite their light casualties, Palo Duro was a catastrophic defeat for the Indians. The historian Dee Brown wrote about Palo Duro in his seminal work *Bury My Heart at Wounded Knee* (1971), one of the first attempts to give the Indians' side of the story of the West. Brown wrote that "Mackenzie's troopers stormed up the creek, burning tepees and destroying the Indians' winter supplies. By the end of the day, they rounded up more than a thousand ponies. Mackenzie ordered the animals driven into Tule Valley, and there the Bluecoats slaughtered them, a thousand dead horses left to the circling buzzards." With no homes, no supplies, and no horses, the Indians had no choice. Within days, the Comanche and their allies began to surrender and start the trek back to their reservations, with Quanah Parker one of the last to return. There were skirmishes between Indians and soldiers for several years to come, but the Red River War was effectively won in 1875 at Palo Duro.

By the end of the Red River War, almost all the Indians of the southern plains were on reservations, with 72 of their leaders banished to the military prison at Fort Marion, Florida. General Sheridan called the war on the southern plains "the most successful of any Indian campaign in this country since its settlement by the whites." When it was over, the only buffalo hunters left on the plains were the entrepreneurs intent on killing as many buffalo and selling as many hides as they could. They were so successful that when a friendly Indian agent named P. B. Hunt allowed a party of Comanche to leave the reservation to hunt buffalo on the southern plains in 1878, his well-meaning gesture was pointless: The great herds were gone and the Comanche hunters were forced to butcher several of their horses before returning for good to the reservation.

5

THE CIVIL WAR YEARS AND AFTERMATH

The Great Plains underwent rapid change in the decade encompassing the Civil War as more and more settlers moved west of the Mississippi, pushing aside the short-lived "permanent Indian frontier." In Colorado alone, 30,000 newcomers arrived between the discovery of gold at Pikes Peak in 1859 and the outbreak of the Civil War in 1861. This was the decade when in rapid succession the Pony Express, the telegraph, and the transcontinental railroad bound the country together in ways unimaginable only a few years earlier.

The first to come was the Pony Express. In 1860, relays of riders carried mail the 2,000 miles between Saint Joseph, Missouri, and Sacramento, California, in only eight days. Within 18 months, even this seemed a slow way to get messages from Missouri to California: the telegraph quickly put the Pony Express out of business. Then, in 1869, the transcontinental railroad was completed, and mail and passengers could travel coast to coast in eight days in relative speed, comfort, and safety, traversing the American heartland that fewer and fewer people thought of as the "Great American Desert."

The outbreak of the Civil War in 1861 clearly accelerated the federal government's desire to bring as much land as possible west of the Mississippi into the Union, but Washington's actions also simply recognized that the frontier was being pushed west with startling speed. In 1861, Dakota, Colorado, and Nevada became territories, followed by Arizona and Idaho in 1863, and Montana in 1864. At the same time, new land was officially opened to settlement: in 1862, President Lincoln

The construction of railroads across the West after the Civil War greatly
changed the balance of power, as indicated in this 19th-century drawing.
It shows a few Indians now thoroughly outmanned by the combination
of soldiers, settlers, and technology. *(Library of Congress)*

signed the Homestead Act, which made public land available for settlement. Under the terms of the act, anyone who farmed 160 acres for five
years would own the land free and clear. In the meantime, new western
states were entering the Union, including Kansas in 1861 and Nevada
in 1864.

Virtually all the critical battles of the Civil War took place east of the
Mississippi, and once the Union defeated the Confederacy at the Battle
of Vicksburg in July of 1863, there were only isolated skirmishes in the
West. Almost all regular army regiments had been pulled out of the
West early in the war, leaving military operations against the Indians in
the hands of an estimated 15,000 to 20,000 volunteers. Ill-trained, often
ill-disciplined, the volunteers nonetheless fought hard because they
were usually stationed close to where they lived.

Immediately after secession, the Confederacy negotiated alliances
with the Five Civilized Tribes (the Cherokee, Creek, Choctaw, Chickasaw, and Seminole) who had been resettled in Oklahoma during the
1830s and 1840s. The Confederacy hoped that these Indians would

defend the South's western frontier, and the members of the Five Civilized Tribes hoped to be able to return to their original homes if the South won the war. Cherokee and Cherokee-Chicksaw regiments fought with Confederate soldiers at several battles, including the Battle of Pea Ridge, Arkansas, in March, 1862, a significant Union victory. After that, for the most part, the Plains Indians sat out the Civil War.

Although there was little Indian involvement in the Civil War itself, in 1862 an uprising of Santee Dakota Sioux living in Minnesota took place and was serious enough that President Lincoln took immediate notice. When the president got word of the Dakota uprising and realized that this was no isolated skirmish but a major uprising, he suspected that the Dakota, like the Five Civilized Tribes, had decided to side with the Confederacy. Lincoln was wrong; the Sioux had their own objective: driving out the homesteaders and reclaiming their land.

Communication across
the plains relied on
Pony Express riders
like this man photo-
graphed in 1861.
(National Archives)

The Dakota uprising of August 17 to September 26, 1862, involved the Santee Dakota living along the Minnesota River on a sliver of reservation land some 150 miles long and no more than 10 miles wide. Like most reservation Indians, the Santee received an annuity of cash, food, and goods; in 1862, the annuity usually handed out at the Upper Agency, an army trading post, in early summer still had not been distributed by August. For whatever reason, the money simply had not arrived at the Upper Agency and the Santee had to buy food on credit from the agency traders. The traders, all too familiar with past government inefficiency in distributing the annuity, became increasingly worried that the annuity might never arrive. At that point, they cut off any further credit. When one of the traders, Andrew Myrick, was told that the Indians would soon be in danger of starving, he remarked "Let them eat grass"—a remark which quickly circulated among the Dakota.

On August 4, the Santee Dakota camped at the Upper Agency took matters into their hands and broke into a warehouse where food was stored. While one of the two regiments of Minnesota Volunteers was surrounded by the Indians, the second regiment, under Lieutenant

Thomas Gere, opened fire, and the Indians withdrew. The conflict escalated on August 17.

In yet another incident, an unsuccessful and hungry Dakota hunting party returning to their Minnesota River reservation made off with a clutch of eggs from an isolated farm. The farmer protested, taunts were exchanged, and by nightfall, the Dakota had killed the farmer, Robinson Jones, his wife, daughters, and three nearest neighbors. When the Indian hunting party arrived back at the reservation that evening, the most important chiefs, Red Middle Voice and Little Crow, agreed not to hand them over to the authorities. Most of the Dakota felt that, with so many farmers off fighting in the Civil War, this was the ideal time to mount an all-out assault to drive out the settlers.

Although Little Crow warned that there were too many settlers and too few Dakota, his words were greeted with considerable suspicion because he had converted to Christianity and lived in a wooden house. Could his judgment, the others wonder, be trusted, or had he gone over to the enemy? In the end, the Dakota decided to attack both the Upper and Lower Agencies, less than a day's march apart, as a preliminary step to wiping out the farm settlements. Little Crow, his objections overruled, went on the warpath with his people. As one of the Dakota warriors, Lightning Blanket, later recalled, "The young men were all anxious to go and we dressed as warriors in war paint, breechclouts and leggings, with a large sash around us to keep our food and ammunition in."

The attack on the Lower Agency was a success, and the agency had to be evacuated, with some traders escaping by ferryboat across the Minnesota River to Fort Ridgely. Trader Andrew Myrick, who had suggested that the Indians eat grass, was killed and left with his mouth stuffed with grass. The Indians next attacked isolated farms and settlements up and down the river valley, killing 50 German settlers in one hamlet alone, and entire families on small homesteads. When 48 soldiers under Capt. John Marsh set out from Fort Ridgely to relieve the Lower Agency, they were ambushed at the ferry crossing and lost 25 men.

The Indians next attacked the Upper Agency, killing a party of 25 settlers whom they encountered en route, but they did not capture anyone. One woman, Justina Kreiger, saw her husband killed and, although seriously wounded, attempted to save a group of 11 children by hiding them in a wagon. In all, seven children, including six of Mrs. Kreiger's, were saved. As for Justina Kreiger herself, she was found two weeks later by a passing party of soldiers, barely alive and wandering on the prairie.

The Indians next moved south to Fort Ridgely, rightly thinking that if they could capture the fort, they would control the surrounding countryside. On August 22, some 800 Dakota warriors attacked the fort, but were driven back by cannon fire. The Dakota lost some 100 men in the encounter, while only three of the soldiers within Fort Ridgely were killed.

Despite their losses, the Dakota attacked the small town of New Ulm, south of Fort Ridgely, on the banks of the Minnesota River. Families from outlying communities had streamed into New Ulm since the uprising began, doubling its population to almost 2,000. About 500 Dakota attacked early in the day and the fighting went on until dusk, by which time 165 of the town's 190 houses had been burned and 26 of the defenders killed. Fortunately for the survivors, the Indians did not attack the next day, and the survivors were evacuated.

At this point, Minnesota governor Alexander Ramsey attempted to coordinate the counterattack against the Dakota, placing all his forces under former fur trader Henry Sibley. The Dakota, Ramsey stated, "must be exterminated or driven forever beyond the borders of the state." In September, Sibley's combined force of volunteers and regular soldiers decisively defeated the Dakota at the Battle of Wood Lake, south of the Upper Agency. Almost at once, many of the Santee Dakota began to drift out on the plains, leaving behind them some 270 captives, mostly women and children. The six-week-long Eastern Sioux War was over, and although at least 400 Minnesota settlers had been killed, the Santee Dakota had lost, not gained, ground in the conflict. Although no one could have known it at the time, the Santee uprising (which became known as the Minnesota Uprising) was the beginning of the struggle that would end with the final defeat of the Lakota Sioux at Wounded Knee in 1890.

Although the fighting was over, the desire for revenge and punishment remained. The army started to round up those Indians who had not headed out onto the plains, eventually capturing at least 2,000. More than 400 of these Dakota were brought to Fort Ridgely and put on trial; anyone who could be shown to have been present at a battle was automatically given the death penalty. Soon, 300 Indians were condemned to be hanged and moved to a prison at the town of Mankato. There they might all have been executed, had not the Episcopal bishop of Minnesota, Henry Whipple, written to President Lincoln to plead for clemency. Lincoln concurred, and declared that only those guilty of murder or rape should be executed; the others were sent to join Confederate prisoners of war being held at the military prison at Rock Island, Illinois.

On December 26, 38 of the Dakota were hanged in a mass execution and their bodies buried in a shallow communal grave. (This was the largest official mass execution in U.S. history.) Even then, the Dakota were not at rest: a number of local doctors, including William Mayo, who later founded Minnesota's famous Mayo Clinic, had attended the executions. That night, they drew lots, dug up the bodies, and carted off the corpses, which they then converted into skeletons to use as teaching aids.

In all, some 30,000 Minnesota settlers had fled their farms and towns during the Sioux Uprising of 1862. When the fighting was over, many returned home, but others moved on, leaving 23 counties virtually unpopulated. Gradually, Minnesota was resettled; by then, the Santee Dakota were living on the plains, where they joined the Lakota and Nakota Sioux already living there in their attempt to keep the settlers at bay.

Immediately after the Civil War the Lakota Sioux under the great Oglala Lakota war chief Red Cloud, sometimes joined by Arapaho and Cheyenne Indians, began what is variously called the First Sioux War, Red Cloud's War, or the War for the Bozeman Trail (1866–67).

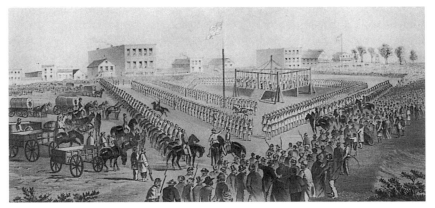

In December 1862, 38 of the Santee Dakota Sioux who had participated in that summer's uprising in Minnesota were hanged in a great public spectacle designed to deliver a message to all American Indians: They had no chance against the armed might of the United States. *(Library of Congress)*

Fort Laramie
FROM TRADING POST
TO NATIONAL HERITAGE SITE

AS THE FIRST EXPLORERS AND SETTLERS MOVED across the Great Plains, they built an elaborate system of missions and forts. The missions were the visible sign of the power of Christianity; the forts were a pointed reminder of the military power first of the European powers colonizing North America and then, after the American Revolution, of the government of the United States. The history of Fort Laramie, in Wyoming, is typical of the forts on the Great Plains. In 1834, two trappers established a trading post, named Fort William, where the Laramie and North Platte Rivers meet. Two years later, a major company, the American Fur Company, bought the fort from its original owners; it was rebuilt and renamed Fort John. As the fur boom diminished but settlers pushed further west, the U.S. Army became interested in acquiring and building forts to protect the settlers from the Indians. In 1849, the U.S. Army took possession of the fort, renamed Fort Laramie, which it held until 1890, when it was officially closed. During this time, Fort Laramie was an important way station on what was often called the Overland (or Oregon) Trail; soldiers from the fort patrolled the trail and protected wagon trains. In 1850, some 50,000 settlers paused here on their way west. Although Laramie never had a wooden stockade or earthen barricade, it was a vital post for the U.S. Army during the Plains Indians Wars. The fort had its own hospital, bakery, barracks, officer's quarters, stables, guardhouse, and trading post. Today, Fort Laramie is administered by the National Park Service (see http://www.npca.org for more information on this, and other National Park Service sites) as a memorial to the importance of the forts that once guarded fur trade, wagon trails, and settlements on the Great Plains.

In 1862–63, gold prospector John Bozeman had found a shortcut from Montana to the Rocky Mountains of Colorado, where gold had been discovered. The U.S. Army immediately realized the importance of the shortcut and decided to fortify a string of outposts along the trail, even though a series of treaties had assigned the land to the Sioux.

In the summer of 1866, under orders from the Commander of the Division of the Mississippi, Gen. William T. Sherman, Col. Henry Carrington led some 700 soldiers of the Second Battalion of the Eighteenth Infantry, accompanied by many of their families and at least 1,000 farm animals, from Old Fort Kearny in Nebraska to Fort Reno, the southernmost fort on the Bozeman Trail. Leaving some of his company to garrison Fort Reno, Carrington headed north to the chosen site of the next fort, just east of the Bighorn Mountains on the Powder River. There, Carrington began to build Fort Phil Kearny, named after a Civil War hero. Two days later, Red Cloud's forces attacked, and from that day until it was abandoned in 1868, Fort Phil Kearny was under virtually constant siege.

In November, a company of cavalry under Capt. William Fetterman and Capt. James Powell arrived at Fort Phil Kearny to help in its defense. Fetterman had not fought Indians before, which may explain why he remarked upon arriving at Fort Kearny that if he had just 80 men, he could "ride through the whole Sioux nation." During the next month, Fetterman fumed as Red Cloud led attacks on every wagon train that made its way along the Lodge Ridge Trail to the fort. Although Carrington always counterattacked, Fetterman felt that the soldiers should seize the initiative.

On December 21, a wagon train making its way along the Lodge Ridge Trail was attacked, and Fetterman got Carrington's permission to relieve the attack. "Under no circumstances," Carrington ordered Fetterman, "pursue over Lodge Ridge Trail." For whatever reason, Fetterman ignored his commander's orders; his entire company of some 80 men was killed when they galloped after a small decoy party of Indians beyond Lodge Ridge Trail to where the main body of Lakota were waiting in ambush. As was often the case, the Lakota did not follow up on their victory and mount an all-out assault on the fort, but Carrington took no chances and evacuated all the women and children south to Fort Reno as soon as possible.

When General Sherman heard what had happened to Fetterman, he immediately dubbed it a massacre and said that the army must "act with vindictive earnestness against the Sioux, even to their extermination, men, women, and children." Fighting raged up and down the Bozeman Trail for the next two years, with the Sioux concentrating their attacks on the three forts; Fetterman himself was honored by having a fort named after him. By 1868, Sherman realized that exterminating the Sioux was going to be harder than he had thought.

In April of 1868, a peace commission sent out from Washington met with many of the Sioux at Fort Laramie; Red Cloud refused to attend, as did the three Lakota chiefs who would play important roles in the struggle that led to Little Big Horn: Sitting Bull, Crazy Horse, and Gall. Those Sioux who did sign the Treaty of Fort Laramie were given South Dakota as their exclusive reservation homeland. In addition, they received assurances that they could continue to hunt in their ancestral hunting grounds east of the Bighorn Mountains in the Powder River country of southern Montana. In May, the three forts on the Bozeman Trail were abandoned and almost immediately torched by the Sioux. At that point, Red Cloud himself came to Fort Laramie and agreed to live in peace with the whites. The War of the Bozeman Trail had ended— and the Sioux were the victors.

Like so many treaties before it, the 1868 Treaty of Fort Laramie only interrupted, but did not end, hostilities. President U. S. Grant threw

In the spring of 1868, General Sherman headed a "peace commission" that signed a treaty with the Sioux at Fort Laramie. It effectively recognized that the Sioux had won the so-called Red Cloud's War over the Bozeman Trail, but the treaty would soon be ignored. Sherman is the dark-bearded man to the left of the center pole. *(National Archives)*

himself behind the efforts of American Quakers and their supporters in Congress in the "Indian Peace Party" to put a lasting end to hostilities on the plains. In 1870, Red Cloud himself visited Washington to put the Indian case to the "Great White Father." Red Cloud was wined and dined in Washington, where he attended a banquet at the White House at which President Grant urged him to become a farmer, which Red Cloud regarded as a willful insult. After Red Cloud returned home, things were quiet for a while, but further conflict between the Lakota and the government was inevitable.

As the frontier moved west, so did the railroads. In the spring of 1873, engineers of the Northern Pacific railroad, accompanied by more than 1,500 soldiers under the command of Col. D. S. Stanley, forged deep into Indian territory in the Yellowstone Valley to scout out the best route for the new line across Montana. One of Stanley's company commanders was the young Civil War hero Col. George A. Custer. Unlike many in the military, Stanley was not favorably impressed by Custer, whom he described as a "cold-blooded, untruthful, and unprincipled man." Only the Panic of 1873, in which prominent railroad backer Jay Cooke lost much of his fortune, kept work from beginning immediately on the Northern Pacific line, which would have cut through land guaranteed to the Indians in the Treaty of Fort Laramie.

The next year, General Sheridan evidently decided that there was too large a gap between Fort Abraham Lincoln on the upper Missouri and Fort Ellis, near Bozeman, Montana. Sheridan sent Custer and 10 companies of the Seventh Cavalry on a scouting mission into the Black Hills, which the Indians called Pasapa, to determine where best to build a new fort. In so doing, Sheridan ignored the fact that the Black Hills were in the heart of the Lakota territory described in the Treaty of Fort Laramie as the unceded Indian territory "north of the North Platte River and east of the summits of the Big Horn Mountains."

Sheridan also ignored the fact that the Black Hills were the most sacred spot on Earth for the Sioux. According to legend, their ancestors had been born in the Wind Cave high up in the Black Hills, whose rugged contours mirrored the all-important Buffalo Constellation in the sky above. All the most important Sioux ceremonies, including the Sun Dance each June, were held in the Black Hills.

Custer's expedition was not just looking for a good fort site: Several geologists traveled with him, looking for gold. Custer was so excited by the geologists' preliminary reports that he sent a scout dashing off to

Gen. Philip Sheridan, depicted here on horseback in battle, sent General Custer to look for a new fort site and gold in the Black Hills—ignoring this land's significance to the Lakota. *(Library of Congress, Prints and Photographs Division [LC-USZ62-101469])*

Fort Laramie with the news that gold had been found in the Black Hills. When the news reached Fort Laramie, and was sent out from there by telegraph, a new gold rush was on. In fact, the first prospectors arrived in the Black Hills before Custer and his expedition had time to make their way back to Fort Abraham Lincoln.

Initially, General Sherman ordered the prospectors to leave the Black Hills, but they paid as much attention to him as he had to the Treaty of Fort Laramie. As word of the influx of prospectors spread among the Lakota during 1875, more and more Indians left the reservation and headed into the Black Hills. At that point, the government attempted to clear the way to develop the Black Hills by offering to buy the land from the Lakota. After Chief Red Cloud asked for the astronomical sum of $600 million, Washington ordered that all the Sioux, not just those who had signed the Treaty of Fort Laramie, leave the Black Hills and make their way to the Great Sioux Reservation in South Dakota by January 31. When the Sioux and their Cheyenne allies ignored the order, General Sheridan prepared for all-out war on the northern plains. In March, Sheridan sent out three columns of his best troops, made up of about 2,650 men, in a pincer attack to converge on where he thought the main body of Sioux were located, near the convergence of the Yellowstone and Bighorn Rivers in Montana. The campaign that followed initiated the last great war between the Indians and the U.S. Army on the northern plains.

6

SOLDIER AND
SETTLER

Life During the
Plains Indian Wars

During the last half of the 19th century, the Indians were confronted primarily by two groups of Americans: the settlers and the U.S. Army. Allied against the Indians, the settlers and the army nonetheless frequently found themselves coexisting in uneasy harmony. Often the soldiers regarded the settlers as innocents who were always getting themselves into trouble with the Indians, while the settlers regarded the soldiers as roughnecks and rowdies. Sometimes problems arose because, as George Custer's wife Libby politely put it in *Boots and Saddles,* her memoir of life on the plains between 1873 and 1876, the army was a "medley of incongruous elements." An article in the *New York Sun* in 1877 put it less politely: "The Regular Army is composed of bummers, loafers, and foreign paupers."

During the Civil War, the U.S. Army had been made up of a broad cross section of the population, as volunteers from all walks of life enlisted to fight for the Union. This changed radically after the war: now the volunteers were largely out-of-work laborers who saw military service as an escape from civilian woes. As many as half the new recruits between 1865 and 1874 were recent Irish and German immigrants, many illiterate and almost all unskilled.

This sketch by Frederic Remington (ca. 1888) shows a group of "Buffalo Soldiers," African-American cavalrymen, on duty in the American West with the famous Tenth Cavalry. *(Library of Congress)*

The soldiers in the new army were notoriously ill trained: some of the cavalry had never sat on a horse before enlisting. Many were hard drinkers. So many deserted that General Sherman jested that there was no need to worry about peopling the plains because the deserters would make more than enough settlers. Still, some of the men in this incongruous medley were excellent soldiers and went on to become officers. In 1874, 13 percent of all officers had been commissioned from the ranks, and 87 of 193 officers commissioned from the ranks were of foreign birth.

One group in the army had almost no deserters: the African Americans, whose desertion rate was the lowest in U.S. military history. Immediately after the Civil War, after much debate, it had been decided that two of the cavalry and four of the infantry regiments would be made up of African-American soldiers commanded by white officers. Despite the excellent performance of 175,000 black soldiers in the Civil War, much of the military establishment remained skeptical of their worth as soldiers and absolutely opposed to black officers commanding black soldiers.

By and large, the African-American soldiers saw in the army, despite its segregation and prejudice, a possibility for steady work. Virtually all the African-American soldiers served in the West, where they were nicknamed "Buffalo Soldiers" by the Plains Indians. Theories vary as to the genesis of the nickname, with some historians suggesting that the Indians thought that the black soldiers fought with the strength of the buffalo. Other historians have suggested that the African-American soldiers' hair reminded the Indians of the thick, black buffalo's mane.

Life in the army was particularly difficult for the Buffalo Soldiers. The African-American Tenth Cavalry, stationed at Fort Leavenworth, Kansas, was assigned to down-at-the-heels quarters in a swampy section of the fort grounds and issued inferior uniforms, weapons, and horses. Despite these inequities, the men of the Tenth acquitted themselves well in skirmishes with the Cheyenne and Apache. In the campaign against the great Apache chief Geronimo in 1886, Sgt. William McBrayar became the first black soldier to win the Congressional Medal of Honor.

When the Civil War ended in 1865, Congress had been faced with the job of deciding how to redefine and reorganize the army, which had swollen to more than 1 million during the war. The Army Act of 1866 described the role of the post–Civil War army as threefold: reconstructing the South, protecting the coasts, and defending the western frontier. The new army, like the old, was comprised of administrative (known as staff) and fighting (known as line) branches. The line army was set at 54,000 men. This was far fewer than during the Civil War, but considerably larger than the pre–Civil War army of 18,000 men—and too large for the tastes of some in Congress. By 1874, a series of congressional acts had pruned the army to 27,000, with 10 cavalry regiments, 25 infantry regiments, and eight artillery regiments. The frontier army was also authorized to hire up to 1,000 Indian scouts.

The cavalry and artillery regiments were composed of 12 companies, with 10 companies in each infantry regiment. In theory, each company would have 100 men, but companies were often well below strength. In 1877, the Seventh Infantry fought the Battle of the Big Hole with an average of only 24 men in each company. At best, General Sheridan had only 1,200 cavalrymen and 1,200 infantrymen at his disposal to maintain order across the 150,000 square miles of the vast Department of the Missouri.

The Weapons That Took the West

THE MOST IMPORTANT FIREARMS DURING THE PERIOD of the Plains Indian Wars were the Springfield rifle, the Winchester repeating rifle, the Colt .45, the Gatling gun, and the Hotchkiss two-pound machine gun. These weapons had two things in common: They could fire rapidly and were easily portable. Perhaps the most famous small arm at the time of the Plains Indians Wars was the Colt .45, with its revolving cylinder that allowed it to fire repeatedly without being reloaded before each shot. Samuel Colt did not invent the revolving cylinder, but he perfected it and patented it. The Colt .45 (nicknamed the "Peacemaker," for its deadly accuracy) became famous during the U.S.-Mexican War, when Samuel Colt got an order from the U.S. Army for 1,000 pistols. Thereafter, the Colt .45 was the standard-issue pistol of the army. The gun was so popular, that "Colt" became the slang term used simply to mean any pistol. Another very popular gun was the lightweight, rapid-fire Winchester rifle; the U.S. Army often resisted issuing the Winchester to its troops, fearing that its ease of firing might lead to a waste of ammunition. Similar concerns did not stop the army from adopting the lightweight rapid-fire Gatling gun, a prototype of the machine gun used in World War I. Ironically, these weapons, which settlers and soldiers used against the Plains Indians, also profoundly transformed the Indians' own warfare. Although the Plains Indians traded buffalo pelts to gunrunners for firearms and acquired weapons by raids on wagon trains and settlements, they were never able to obtain enough firearms to fight the settlers and the U.S. Army on equal terms. Nonetheless, the original Indian concept of daring raids executed to count coup and win glory was replaced by the European-American concept of all-out war—a fight to the finish—for territory and power. It was, of course, a fight the Plains Indians lost.

Sheridan's Department of the Missouri was one of a number of administrative units that the Army Act of 1866 had established for the territory west of the Mississippi. The Division of the Missouri contained the Department of the Missouri (Missouri, Kansas, Colorado, and New Mexico), the Department of the Platte (Iowa, Nebraska, Utah, and parts of Dakota and Montana), the Department of Dakota (Minnesota and parts of Dakota and Montana), and the Department of

Arkansas (Indian Territory). The Pacific Division contained the Department of California (California, Nevada, and Arizona), while the Department of Columbia oversaw Oregon, Washington, and Idaho. Texas was administered by the Division of the Gulf.

The post–Civil War years were no exception to the general rule that army pay is never generous: a private earned $13 a month, a line sergeant made $22, and a colonel took home $300. In addition, living conditions in the frontier forts were primitive. Soldiers' journals are full of references to louse-infested bunks and maggot-ridden food. Salt pork, beans, and hardtack (a hard bread or biscuit) appeared at most meals, and dysentery and scurvy were endemic. Frequent plagues of grasshoppers made fresh vegetables and fruits scarce. One soldier recorded in his journal that in the summer of 1873 at Fort Rice, Dakota, "The damn hoppers came along, by God, and ate my garden, by God, then the birds ate the hoppers, by God, and we killed and ate the birds, by God, so that we were even in the long run, by God."

The extreme variations in temperature so characteristic of the Great Plains made life particularly difficult for those stationed here. In *Boots and Saddles,* Elizabeth Custer wrote of winters at Fort Lincoln, North Dakota, when "from 20 to 30 degrees below zero was ordinary weather" and "there was no lumber at the post except unseasoned cottonwood."

Testimony to the fact that at least some officers at times enjoyed "the good life" at frontier posts is this picture (ca. 1873) showing officers' families playing croquet at Fort Bridger, Wyoming Territory. *(National Archives)*

A portrait of George and Elizabeth Custer with an unidentified man. *(National Archives)*

There was no well on the fort, and soldiers had to fill the water wagon by digging through the five feet of ice on a nearby river. When the temperature went down to 45 degrees below zero, Mrs. Custer recorded that "the utmost vigilance" had to be practiced to keep sentinels, wrapped in buffalo robes, from freezing to death. Things were no better in summer, when the plains baked under the sun and mosquitoes swarmed through layers of protective clothing—which in Mrs. Custer's case included a head net, waterproof cloak, buckskin gauntlets, and several layers of newspaper stuffed into her knee-high riding boots.

Even General Sherman spoke harshly of life on the plains, writing in 1874 that "some of what are called military posts are mere collections of huts of logs, adobes, or mere holes in the ground, and are about as much 'forts' as prairie dog villages might be called 'forts.'" Forts in the most vulnerable positions—like Fort Phil Kearny in the Dakota territory—were built with high stockade fences, but many garrisons were built without defensive walls, and looked like simple villages. The parade ground took the place of the village green and was flanked by barracks for the enlisted men, houses for the officers, stables for the horses, and various outbuildings, including the company store, laundry rooms (known as "Suds Row"), and the canteen—where serious drinking and gambling often took place.

Although officers could bring their wives and families (and even servants) along to many postings, an enlisted man who wanted to bring along his wife had to wait until there was an opening for a position as one of the four company laundresses. In general, distinctions of rank were strictly maintained, but at great events, such as Christmas dinner or dances, the ranks mingled. When the Custers were at Fort Lincoln, each company gave a winter ball in a barracks cleared of its bunks, decorated with flags, and lit by candles. The regimental band, which often accompanied the soldiers into action, played a medley of quadrilles and waltzes. The women wore their finest attire (Mrs. Custer found some of the laundresses' outfits a bit flamboyant) and the men, of course, were in uniform. At one ball, the banquet featured what Mrs. Custer later recorded as two great luxuries: fresh cake and a potato salad flavored with hard-to-find onions.

Such scenes of life on the post were later immortalized in John Ford's westerns such as *Fort Apache* and *She Wore a Yellow Ribbon,* whose cast of characters includes the bibulous Irish master sergeant, the officers' wives and sweethearts, the sturdy laundress with a heart of gold, and the handsome young officers in their smart dark blue uniforms.

In fact, there was considerable flexibility in the uniforms worn both by enlisted men and officers. Custer himself designed much of what he wore, from fringed buckskins to more ornate versions of the traditional dark blue army officer's jacket and trousers. Enlisted men were issued uniforms, usually ill fitting; if they wanted their clothes to fit, soldiers had to pay the regimental tailor for alterations. Even then, the cloth used in the uniforms was widely regarded as being too heavy for summer, too light for winter—and too cheap to last.

On parade and for dress occasions, infantry and cavalry officers wore elaborate helmets, some with horsehair plumes. In combat, most men wore, as one soldier wrote, "white hats, brown hats, black hats, all kinds of hats except the Service hat." Similarly, men in the same company might wear shirts and trousers in a variety of colors and materials. A reporter for *The New York Times* wrote in 1876 of a column of Fifth Cavalry that "about the only things in their dress which marked them as soldiers were their striped pants and knee boots, both well besplattered with mud." The yellow stripe on the cavalry men's pants won them the nickname "Yellowlegs."

There was a good deal more uniformity in the men's weapons than in their clothing. Cavalrymen continued to be issued sabers, but new rifles and pistols were the weapon of choice. The various Civil War powder-and-ball muskets had been converted into breech-loading rifles that fired bullets. The most reliable rifle was the Springfield Allin, manufactured in Springfield, Massachusetts, and used throughout the army from about 1873 until the end of the century. Similarly, old-style pistols were replaced by bullet-firing pistols, notably the Colt .45 single-action revolver known as the "Peacemaker." Another new weapon, the Winchester repeating rifle, was not standard army issue—although the Plains Indians soon realized its worth and it became the Sioux weapon of choice in combat.

The post–Civil War years also saw advances in artillery weapons: the Hotchkiss two-pounder machine gun was reliable up to 4,000 yards and light enough to be taken into the field easily. The Gatling gun, a prototype of the machine gun, fired an impressive 350 rounds of rifle ammunition a minute, but often overheated and jammed. Consequently, many commanders, including George Custer at the Little Big Horn, chose not to use them.

In the years after the Civil War, just as new technology changed the weapons used by the army patrolling the Great Plains, technological advances also radically changed civilian life there. The transcontinental railroad was finished in 1869, and by 1883, when the Southern Pacific railroad linked New Orleans, Louisiana, and San Francisco, and the Northern Pacific railroad linked Saint Paul, Minnesota, and Portland, Oregon, a network of rail lines cut through the Great Plains. The railroad meant that instead of a steady trickle of settlers moving west by covered wagon and stagecoach, homesteaders poured into the plains on trains. Many, indeed, homesteaded land sold by the rail companies and soon, what one newcomer called "mushroom western towns" sprouted along the rail lines.

The white population on the plains grew at an astonishing rate. A considerable number of former slaves from Kentucky, Missouri, Mississippi, and Tennessee also moved west after the Civil War, many settling in Denver and others founding all-black communities such as Nicodemus, Kansas.

The end of the Civil War also meant the resumption and expansion of the Great Plains cattle industry. The Texas cattle industry, neglected

Note how this Nebraska family added several touches (including bird cages) that converted a typically basic 19th-century sod house into a true home. *(Library of Congress)*

during the war, picked up almost immediately. At first, most cattle were driven from Texas to Saint Joseph and Sedalia, Missouri, and then shipped east to Saint Louis and Chicago. Soon, new trails were opened, and great herds were driven north along the Shawnee Trail from San Antonio to Kansas City, while others made the journey along the Goodnight-Loving Trail from Texas north to Denver, Colorado, and on to Wyoming and Montana. The increased number of settlers, combined with the presence of the army, and the need for beef to distribute to reservation Indians created a boom market for cattle. At the same time, "cow towns," from which beef was shipped east by freight train, sprang up on the Great Plains.

Between 1867 and 1871, as many as 300,000 cattle were driven each year from Texas to the first great cow town, Abilene, Kansas, from which most were shipped east for slaughter. During those years, Abilene was a notoriously lawless, saloon-infested town, and its inhabitants had to enlist marshals such as Tom Smith and Wild Bill Hickok to establish some semblance of law and order. Things got so bad that the Abilene Farmers' Protective Association banned the cattle drives from town, whereupon the cowboys took their business to Wichita and Dodge City.

The conflict between the farmers and the cowboys in Abilene was to be repeated across the Great Plains in the years to come. No farmer wanted herds of cattle stripping his land; no cowman wanted to find a farmer's fences in his way. By the late 1880s, overgrazing on the plains had tipped the balance in the direction of the homesteaders and farmers. The Great Plains could no longer support the great migratory herds of cattle, and the cattle boom was over. Farmers, using new inventions like the Oliver chilled plow (1868) and automatic seeders (1874), were putting more and more land into cultivation, fencing it with another new invention, barbed wire (1874), and watering it with the powerful windmill pump invented in Connecticut by Daniel Halliday in 1854.

Across the Great Plains, settlers in towns near the rail lines often lived in houses made of wood brought in from the East, but out on the prairie, most settlers lived in primitive dugouts cut into the ground or sod houses made from sod strips cut from the prairie itself. The thick roots of the prairie grass held the sod together and made it a serviceable substitute for bricks. These sod houses were not very different from the earthen lodges that such tribes as the Mandan, whom George Catlin painted, had lived in for so many generations. Like the Indians, the early homesteaders collected buffalo chips to use as fuel. With the disappearance of the buffalo in the 1880s, first cow chips and then coal, imported from the East, were used.

Homesteaders and Indians on the plains regarded each other with justifiable suspicion across an almost unbridgeable gulf, as even two simple stories reveal. Homesteader Agnes Milner kept a journal of her family's journey to Colorado and recorded that "twice during the trip Indians were determined that my father should trade my mother for some of their ponies." Milner's opinion of the Native Americans she met did not improve when she settled in Colorado. The Indians, she wrote, "were always stealing everything they could get their hands on, but their specialties were soap, sugar, and blueing." At about the same time that Agnes Milner was keeping her journal, Big Eagle, a Santee Dakota, dictated his memoirs to newspaperman Return I. Holdombe. "The whites," he stated, "always seemed to say by their manner when they saw an Indian, 'I am much better than you.'" And yet, Big Eagle complained, white men often mistreated Indian women, a sure sign that whites were inferior beings.

Bit by bit, homesteaders were conquering the challenge of the Great Plains, although most lived in conditions almost as austere as those endured by the U.S. Army in its frontier forts. Women were idealized by men on the plains as being a civilizing influence on life there. Of course, not every frontier woman was a plucky army wife or energetic homesteader, a school teacher or missionary. The Great Plains had its share of prostitutes, and more than its share of characters like Calamity Jane, who lived the life of a hard-drinking cowhand. Calamity Jane was an extreme case, but many women found increased freedom in the West. At a time when a woman living on her own "back East" was regarded with considerable suspicion, in some sections of the plains as many as 15 percent of the homesteaders were single women.

Mountain Men

THE MOUNTAIN MEN WERE ORIGINALLY FUR TRAPPERS and traders who trapped beaver in the rivers and streams of the Rocky Mountains. The heyday of the mountain men was brief; the first expedition into the Rockies to trap beaver took place in 1822, the last in the 1840s. But no non-Indian knew the routes across the mountains and plains better than they did, and many of them became the guides to explorers, military parties, and settlers. Their lasting fame was jump-started in the 1830s and 1840s by the novels of James Fenimore Cooper and the paintings of Albert Jacob Miller. Cooper's flinty hero Natty Bumppo, nicknamed Leatherstocking, was modeled on such real mountain men as Kit Carson. The fictional Leatherstocking was one of the nation's first literary heroes to be cast in the mold of the rugged individualist. Miller's paintings created romantic images of a frontiersman who was himself as much of a "noble savage" as the Indians he encountered. The reality was, as always, less romantic: The mountain men lived most of the year in isolated, primitive conditions. Once or twice a year, they brought their furs to trading posts, such as Fort Laramie, where they traded the pelts, had a shave and a bath, and drank considerable amounts of whiskey. What did in the mountain men was a change in fashions: When beaver top hats went out of style in the late 1830s, the mountain men took their place in the mythology of the Old West.

A teacher and her class stand in front of their sod schoolhouse in Oklahoma Territory. Many young women went to the frontier to serve as
teachers, then stayed to marry and raise their own families.
(National Archives)

Just as Libby Custer's *Boots and Saddles* gives a clear picture of army
life on the plains, countless letters sent home to relatives back East and
journals written to pass lonely hours record the homesteaders' daily life.
Flora Spiegelberg, who called herself "the first Jewish woman in New
Mexico," wrote an account of her life in Santa Fe in the 1880s. Mrs.
Spiegelberg's reminiscences included seeing the notorious outlaw Billy
the Kid buy a suit at her husband's dry-goods store, founding a religious
school for the eight local Jewish children, and becoming good friends
with the Catholic archbishop. Another early settler, Mrs. W. B. Caton,
years later recalled setting out for Kansas in 1879, with "a wagon, three
horses, and our humble household necessities—bound for the
Promised Land." Like thousands of others, when she arrived, she
thought that "instead of the Wild West, we had found God's own country, and we were quite content to accept it as our future home." Like
most settlers, Mrs. Caton was untroubled that her future home was the
ancestral home of the Indians, even then engaged in their final struggle
to retain control of the Great Plains.

7
CUSTER, SITTING BULL, AND THE BATTLE OF LITTLE BIGHORN

When the Sioux and their allies ignored U.S. government orders to return to the Great Sioux Reservation by January 31, 1876, General Sheridan soon resolved to wage all-out war against the Indians on the northern plains. Although the war would be fought more or less constantly until 1890, the most famous battle took place in June of 1876: the Battle of Little Bighorn, which pitted Chiefs Sitting Bull, Gall, and Crazy Horse against George Custer.

In 1876, General Sheridan, commander of the Division of the Missouri, was particularly worried because of reports that increasing numbers of Indians were leaving the reservations. In fact, the reports seriously underestimated the number of Indians involved. By May, as many as 15,000 Sioux and their allies were converging on the Yellowstone River Valley for the annual celebration of the Sun Dance, and with the hope of resuming their traditional way of life on the plains. The Sioux were also intent on protecting the sacred Black Hills from exploitation.

To combat the northern plains Indians, Sheridan decided to employ a variant of the three-pronged pincer campaign that had been so effective in dividing and conquering during the war on the southern plains in 1874. In May, Sheridan sent Gen. George Crook and his 1,000 men north from Fort Fetterman toward the Yellowstone Valley in Montana. At the same time, Brig. Gen. Alfred Terry led 1,200 men, including

Custer's Seventh Cavalry, west from Fort Abraham Lincoln toward the Yellowstone while Col. John Gibbon moved his 450 men east toward the Yellowstone from Fort Ellis in western Montana. Sheridan's plan was that each of the three columns would search out, engage, and defeat the Indians—and force any survivors back onto the reservation. The three columns would meet up along the Yellowstone, where all Sheridan's reports suggested that the Lakota Sioux, including their three greatest chiefs, Gall, Crazy Horse, and Sitting Bull, were gathering for the summer Sun Dance.

This photograph (ca. 1885) of Sitting Bull captures the ambivalence Americans felt about Indians. He is portrayed here as a dignified chief—yet in five years, felt to be a threat, he would be killed. *(National Archives)*

The Lakota were exceptionally fortunate to have these three chiefs as their leaders in 1876. Gall, a militarily brilliant Hunkpapa Lakota, had so distinguished himself in Red Cloud's War that Sitting Bull adopted him as a younger brother. Gall was consistently opposed to any accommodation with the whites, such as the Treaty of Fort Laramie of 1868. A brilliant leader in battle, Gall was the Hunkpapa Lakota war chief. As for Sitting Bull, he was known for his strength, personal courage, and determination to halt the advance of the settlers on the Great Plains. In addition, Sitting Bull was a renowned medicine man whose visions were both respected and trusted by his people. The third Lakota leader, Crazy Horse, an Oglala-Brute Lakota, was perhaps the greatest of the three: he fought in virtually every important Lakota battle from the Fetterman Fight in 1866 to Little Bighorn in 1876 and never received a wound. Like Sitting Bull, he was a man of visions, but of the two, he was the greater warrior.

These three—Gall, Sitting Bull, and Crazy Horse—led the Lakota whom General Sheridan planned to trap with his three-pronged attack. In early June of 1876, the troops led by General Terry and by Colonel

Gibbon, after uneventful marches, met near the mouth of the Rosebud River, which feeds into the Yellowstone. As Terry and Gibbon pitched camp, the third expedition commander, General Crook, making his way north along the Rosebud, was about to see battle. A West Point graduate and Civil War veteran, and a veteran of the campaign against the Apache, Crook was the man Sherman called the "greatest Indian fighter the United States ever had." Now he was about to engage in the first battle in the last major war between the Indians and the U.S. Army.

On June 15, 1876, Crook led his 20 companies of some 1,050 men toward the Rosebud, which took its name from the profusion of wild roses that grew along its banks. Crook's scouts had reported a major Sioux encampment somewhere along the Rosebud and they were right: on the evening of June 16, Crazy Horse and Sitting Bull sent a note to Crook saying "Come so far, but no farther; cross the river at your peril."

Despite this warning, in the early morning hours of June 17, Crook led his men across the Rosebud in an attack on a Lakota force at least twice as large. Crook could not know that only a week earlier, the Lakota had held a Sun Dance nearby that had lasted for several days. At that time, Sitting Bull had cut 100 pieces of flesh from his chest and arms and had a vision in which he saw white soldiers falling headfirst into his camp. This omen raised the morale of the Lakota and their Cheyenne allies and may help to explain what happened in the Battle of the Rosebud.

When Crook and his soldiers attacked, the Indians, who clearly were ready and waiting, stood and fought a concerted action, rather than using their usual "feint, attack, and withdraw" style of combat. Sitting Bull, still weakened from his self-inflicted wounds, seems to have concentrated on making good medicine during the battle, while Crazy Horse fought fiercely, calling out to his warriors, "Come on, Dakotas, it's a good day to die." Although hand-to-hand combat raged from early morning to midafternoon, when the Indians finally withdrew from the field, each side had lost only about 10 men— the number of wounded, however, was considerable for both the U.S. Army and the Indians.

One of Crook's officers, Capt. Anson Mills, later wrote of the fight that "these Indians were most hideous, everyone being painted in most hideous colors and designs, stark naked, except their moccasins, breech clouts and head gear, the latter consisting of feathers and horns . . . In charging up towards us they exposed little of their person, hanging on with one arm around the neck and one leg over the horse, firing and lancing from underneath the horses' necks, so that there was no part of the Indian at which we could aim."

When the Indians withdrew, Crook claimed victory, but he would have been more honest to say that he avoided defeat. This is why, to this day, some accounts of the Battle of the Rosebud label it a victory for the U.S. Army, some a defeat. After the battle, Crook moved south, sending his wounded by wagon train to Fort Fetterman. As for the Lakota, they headed north, toward the Little Bighorn, where an enormous concentration of Indians was already camped. At the Battle of the Rosebud, the Lakota had learned that they could meet, and withstand, a better-armed U.S. Army force—something that they would remember on June 25, when they met George Custer and the Seventh Cavalry 35 miles away at the Battle of the Little Bighorn.

On June 21, General Terry met with his staff on his supply boat and mobile command post, the riverboat *Far West*, which was docked near the point where the Powder and Yellowstone Rivers converge. Again, the plan was to divide and conquer. Custer was to march along the Rosebud and approach the Little Bighorn River from the south. Terry and Gibbon would take a different route and enter the Little Bighorn Valley from the north. When Custer, Terry, and Gibbon met at the Little Bighorn, they would surround and trap the Indians Terry's scouts had reported to be camped there.

George Armstrong Custer has been called an "American original." After graduating at the bottom of his West Point class in 1861, he became the youngest general in the Union army in 1863. Throughout the Civil War, "Custer's Luck" was famous: He was always at the right place at the right time, right down to Appomattox, where he was present at the surrender. Later, his superior and admirer, General Sheridan, gave him the table on which the surrender was signed. Custer followed his distinguished Civil War career with a court-martial for leaving his post to visit his beloved wife, Libby, in 1867; after a one-year suspension, he rejoined his regiment. Throughout, Custer's luck somehow held, and by 1876, there were those (including Custer himself) who thought of him as a potential candidate for the presidency. If not the first American to mix unmistakable charisma with overweening hubris, his undeniable courage, good looks, almost irresistible charm, and death in combat when he was only 36 ensured that Americans would be arguing over just who George Armstrong Custer really was long after Little Bighorn.

Lt. Col. George Armstrong Custer, in a typically self-conscious pose (and in his signature fringed buckskin jacket), is shown with his staff, their wives, and some visitors, near Fort Abraham Lincoln in Dakota Territory in 1875. *(National Archives)*

About noon on June 22, Custer, in one of his self-designed uniforms combining buckskins, a military shirt, and a broad-brimmed gray hat, led some 600 men of the Seventh Cavalry out of camp as the trumpets sounded "Boots and Saddles." Custer never traveled without a personal entourage, which usually included an indeterminate number of his favorite hounds and a sprinkling of close relatives. Now, Custer had with him his brother-in-law, Lieutenant Calhoun, his brothers, Capt. Tom Custer and the asthmatic civilian Boston Custer, and a 17-year-old nephew, Autie Reed, along for what Custer had promised would be an exciting summer vacation. In addition, a newspaperman, Mark Kellogg of the New York *Herald,* was traveling with Custer.

Modesty was never Custer's strong suit and he probably assumed that Kellogg's battlefield reporting would add to his already considerable fame as the heroic "Boy General" of the Civil War. Some have even suggested that Custer hoped that Kellogg's eyewitness accounts of a victory over the Indians would stampede the Republicans into offering him a place on the presidential ticket at the national convention, meeting in Saint Louis, Missouri, in July. In taking Kellogg along, Custer was ignoring Sheridan's standing order forbidding reporters from going into the field. But Custer had a long history of deciding which orders he would follow and which he would ignore.

Custer's orders were to march as quickly as possible to the Little Bighorn, locate the Indians, and wait until he was joined by Terry and Gibbon. In a letter to Terry written after the battle, Gibbon wrote that he had made a point of repeating Terry's written orders to Custer as he rode out of camp. "Now, Custer," Terry recalled admonishing the

How the Press Covered the Plains Indian Wars

IT IS NOT SURPRISING THAT MARK KELLOGG, A reporter from the New York *Herald,* was with Custer and the Seventh Cavalry at the Battle of Little Bighorn. If things had turned out differently, Kellogg would have telegraphed news back east of a great victory. Interest in the conflicts on the plains was so intense that even the *Illustrated London News* sent reporters and artists west to produce features for readers in England. Virtually all the journalists who covered the Plains Indians Wars wrote accounts that were fiercely partisan. This was hardly surprising: The reporters lived with the army and inevitably absorbed its prejudices. One notable exception was Elaine Goodale Eastman, a teacher and writer who lived among the Dakota Sioux for many years. Eastman, who married a Mdewakanton-Wahpeton Dakota doctor, Charles Eastman, was virtually unique in her sympathetic view of Indians and their ways of life. Her account of Wounded Knee did much to raise questions among the public as to whether this had been a battle, or, as she saw it, a massacre. Nonetheless, most reporters consistently presented the U.S. Army as heroes, while the Plains Indians were portrayed as ignoble savages. As John Finerty, a reporter for the *Chicago Times,* once said of the Indians, "I detest the race." Finerty was unusual among the reporters covering the Plains Indians Wars in that he almost always had a byline; most reporters filed their stories anonymously and their names are unknown. Finerty also increased his own fame by getting a book out of his experiences: *War-Path and Bivouac* (1890). When Finerty died in 1908, the mayor of Chicago was one of his pallbearers, and the funeral cortege was a mile-long procession of police and former army veterans.

impetuous young general, "Don't be greedy, but wait for us." According to some accounts, Custer merely smiled, waved, and rode off. According to other accounts, Custer replied, "No, I won't"—an answer whose ambiguity was to be remembered after the Battle of the Little Bighorn.

If any of the men with Custer was in doubt as to why one of their leader's nicknames was "Old Iron Butt," their doubts were soon

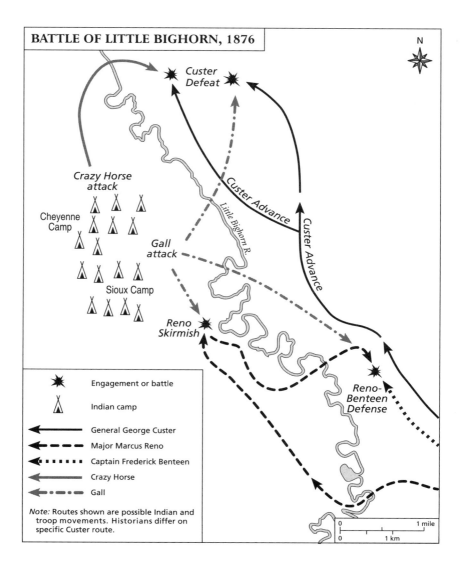

BATTLE OF LITTLE BIGHORN, 1876

N

Custer
Defeat

Crazy Horse
attack

Cheyenne
Camp

Custer Advance

Little Bighorn R.

Custer Advance

Gall
attack

Sioux Camp

Reno
Skirmish

Reno-
Benteen
Defense

Engagement or battle

Indian camp

General George Custer

Major Marcus Reno

Captain Frederick Benteen

Crazy Horse

Gall

Note: Routes shown are possible Indian and troop movements. Historians differ on specific Custer route.

0   1 mile

0   1 km

CUSTER, SITTING BULL, AND THE BATTLE OF LITTLE BIGHORN

This column of cavalry, artillery, and wagons was commanded by Lt. Col. George Custer on an expedition into the Black Hills of Dakota. *(National Archives)*

resolved: After doing an easy 12 miles on June 22, the Seventh made 35 miles on June 23 and a brutal 45 miles on June 24. After resting from 8 P.M. to midnight, Custer, showing no signs of fatigue, gave the orders to move out again. Moving through difficult terrain in utter darkness, the exhausted men of the Seventh covered another 10 miles in five hours before catching a few hours' sleep and resuming their march on the morning of June 25.

At about noon, Custer made the first of a series of decisions that have baffled military historians to this day. Although his scouts were reporting signs of a staggering number of Indians and a large Indian village, Custer divided the Seventh into a supply column and three fighting columns. The three columns were led by Custer himself, Capt. Frederick Benteen, and Maj. Marcus Reno. If Custer had scouting in mind, this was a reasonable tactic, but if he was thinking of engaging the enemy, he had now created three weak fighting forces from one strong regiment. And it was soon clear that Custer intended to fight despite his orders to refrain from doing so.

Custer first ordered Captain Benteen with his three companies to head west to scout out the south fork of the Little Bighorn before heading toward the reported Indian camp on the Little Bighorn itself. After receiving additional confirmation that the Lakota were camped ahead on the Little Bighorn, Custer instructed his adjutant, Lt. W. W. Cooke, to give Major Reno these orders: "General Custer directs you to take as rapid a gait as you think prudent and charge the village, and you will be supported by the whole outfit." As Reno and the second column headed south of the Little Bighorn, Custer ordered another company to drop back and guard the pack mules. Then Custer and his five companies, the third fighting force, headed west on the north side of the river, perhaps intending to attack from the north while Reno pressed up from the south. Whatever Custer's intentions, his actions meant that the Battle of Little Bighorn would be fought as two separate actions: Reno fighting on the south bank of the Little Bighorn and Custer making his last stand on the heights north of the river.

At about 2:30 P.M. on June 25, Reno and his 100 men crossed the Little Bighorn, saw the tipis of a vast Indian village ahead, and opened fire. The Indians seemed to have been caught off guard: It simply had not occurred to them that the vastly outnumbered U.S. Army would attack in the middle of a blazing hot afternoon rather than wait for reinforcements and mount the more traditional dawn attack.

The Indians, however, quickly managed to mount an all-out assault on Reno's troops. After an hour of fierce fighting on the open flats and in the meager cover of a grove of cottonwood trees by the river, Major Reno—splattered by the blood and brains of his favorite Indian scout, Bloody Knife—desperately regrouped his men. Then Reno led his troops in a retreat back across the river and up a debilitatingly steep height to a hill overlooking the Little Bighorn. Later, some would say that Reno had panicked, but his losses were already heavy when he began the retreat.

The Indian attack continued until about 4 P.M., when Captain Benteen and his men, who had made their way west along the South Fork of the Little Bighorn, reached Reno, who gasped, "For God's sake, Benteen, halt your command and help me. I've lost half my men." Reno and Benteen fought on all afternoon, dug in that night, and were attacked again on the morning of June 26. Around midday, as the Indian attack let up, a scout reported that the Indians seemed to be moving camp. The fighting was over and at least 50 of Reno's men lay dead. Reno's relief that the attack was over was overshadowed by his anger at Custer. Where *was* Custer and where was the full support he had promised?

CUSTER, SITTING BULL, AND THE BATTLE OF LITTLE BIGHORN

On the afternoon of June 25, after ordering Reno to charge the Indian village, Custer had continued west for about 12 miles along the barren ridges on the north side of the Little Bighorn, presumably intending to attack the Indians from the north as Reno attacked from the south. When Custer finally saw the enormous Indian village stretched out below him on the south side of the river, he seemed to have realized what his scouts had been telling him all along: this was the largest concentration of Indians ever to confront the U.S. Army. At that point, Custer sent off a messenger to try to locate Benteen and order him to hurry forward with his men and extra ammunition.

Like almost everything about the Battle of Little Bighorn, what happened next is unclear. According to some accounts, Custer galloped forward and opened fire; according to other accounts, Custer and most of his men were almost immediately encircled and attacked. Whoever shot first, by dividing his troops into three fighting columns Custer had first thrust Reno into an almost impossible situation and then placed himself, a handful of civilians, and some 225 cavalrymen in a truly impossible predicament. It did not help that 40 percent of Custer's soldiers were new recruits who had never seen combat before. In about an hour, Custer's Last Stand was all over—and the controversy as to what really happened at Little Bighorn was just beginning.

Probably no battle on American soil, with the possible exception of Gettysburg, has been fought and refought by military historians as many times as the Battle of Little Bighorn. Certainly, no other battle has left such a legacy of unanswered and unanswerable questions. Since Custer and all those with him were killed, the only eyewitness accounts of the battle are those of the Indians who were there that day. One, Jack Red Cloud, the son of the great chief Red Cloud, later gave this account of the battle: "The Sioux kept circling around Custer and as his men came down the ridge we shot them. Then the rest dismounted and gathered in a bunch, kneeling down and shooting from behind their horses."

It is possible to add some details to Jack Red Cloud's scanty account of Little Bighorn from other Indian accounts and from the evidence gathered when a scout with Terry and Gibbon found the battlefield carnage on June 27. In addition, archaeologists have attempted to recreate what happened at Little Bighorn by pinpointing the location of spent ammunition and artifacts on the battlefield. It seems that Custer and his men were strung out for almost three-quarters of a mile along a ridge above the river when they first began to fight. Custer had thought that he would divide and conquer. But on June 25 it was the Indians who did just that, first neutralizing Reno and his men, then cutting Custer's soldiers into small groups and annihilating them one by one.

Chief Gall, who had been active in the fight against Reno, attacked from the southeast, wiping out two entire companies so quickly that the bodies were found almost in platoon formation. Crazy Horse attacked from the southwest, wiping out another three companies. Custer and 51 men retreated up a hill, drew their horses into a circle, shot them, and fought on from behind the protection of their dead mounts until they, too, were dead. Dead, too, were Custer's two brothers, his brother-in-law, young nephew, and the journalist Mark Kellogg, whom Custer had hoped would record his victories against the Plains Indians.

That all those with Custer were killed that day is perhaps the only thing that is absolutely certain about the Battle of Little Bighorn. Some of the Indians at the battle said that Custer died last, firing his pistol to the end—certainly this is the image that passed into popular mythology. Others said that Custer fell near the end, but was not the last to die. At the time of Little Bighorn, Custer had cut the distinctive long reddish-blond curls that made the Indians call him "Hi-es-tzie" or "Long Hair." Consequently, it is not at all clear that the Indians would have

This photograph, taken in 1877, is of the site of "Custer's Last Stand," where only the bones of the horses remain. It is looking toward the ford in Little Bighorn River where the Indians set up their encampment. *(National Archives)*

Chief Gall led the combined Sioux forces in the Battle of Little Bighorn. *(National Archives)*

recognized Custer, although some Lakota later said that Long Hair had not been scalped as a sign of respect. Yet most of the soldiers at Little Bighorn were not scalped, which suggests that Custer was not singled out for any sign of respect. What is known is that when Custer's body was found, his face was peaceful and he had two bullet wounds: one through the heart, the other through his temple.

In later years, Chief Gall often said that the Cheyenne, not the Lakota, had been in the forefront of the fight against Custer—although whether he said this out of modesty, or to avoid blame for the death of one of white America's greatest heroes, no one can say. Sitting Bull gave conflicting accounts of the battle, but recalled that "where the last stand was made, the Long Hair stood like a sheaf of corn with all the ears fallen around him." Crazy Horse, who was famously laconic, said nothing.

After Custer fell, the Lakota renewed their attack on Reno. The fighting continued for much of June 26 until, near sunset, the Indians began to break camp, moving away from the Little Bighorn River into the

Bighorn Mountains. The next morning, Gibbon's Second Cavalry and Seventh Infantry met up with Reno's troops and asked where Custer was. As the troops speculated as to Custer's whereabouts, Lieutenant Bradley, a scout from Terry's column, arrived and announced that he had found Custer and his entire company dead beside the Little Bighorn River.

In the days after Little Bighorn, Reno's wounded were taken to the riverboat *Far West,* which set off for Fort Abraham Lincoln on July 3. The boat, draped with crepe in mourning for Custer and his men, made record time, doing the 700-mile trip to the fort in 54 hours, arriving with the news at 11 P.M. on July 5. There, a telegraph operator spent the next 60 hours sending out word of what was immediately called the Custer Massacre. The news, coming so soon after the July 4 centennial celebrations, shocked the nation. For years, just as with the deaths of President Lincoln, Roosevelt, and Kennedy, people remembered where they were and what they were doing when they got the news of Custer's death. Even President Grant, who remarked openly that Custer had "sacrificed" his men, agreed that Custer's death must be avenged and that the "Indian problem" must now be settled once and for all.

8

FROM LITTLE BIGHORN TO THE GHOST DANCE

The "Custer Massacre," as most Americans called the Battle of Little Bighorn, had both immediate and long-term consequences for the Plains Indians. For much of the next 15 years, the U.S. Army attempted to put an end to the "Indian problem" with a series of small wars directed against virtually all the nonreservation Indians and many of the Native Americans who lived west of the Mississippi on reservations. At the same time that the U.S. Army was attempting to rid the plains of Indians, the U.S. government was enacting sweeping legislation designed to transform Indian territory into new states in the Union.

As word of Custer's defeat spread in July of 1876, the desire for revenge grew. Already in July, General Sheridan had sent Brigadier General Terry, with some 1,600 soldiers, and General Crook, with 2,100 soldiers, into the Rosebud and Yellowstone Valleys to search for the Lakota and Cheyenne who had annihilated Custer. For most of the summer, Terry and Crook's forces operated separately, neither knowing where the other was. More to the point, none of the army scouts, not even the famous Buffalo Bill Cody, could locate the Indians who had been at Little Bighorn.

After the debacle of Little Bighorn, nerves were understandably frayed. On July 23, Crook sent a dispatch to General Sheridan in which he admitted that he was "in constant dread of attack." Sheridan suggested that Crook and Terry meet up and join forces, which they did

Gen. George Crook was one of several men sent to command troops after Custer's defeat. *(National Archives)*

briefly in early August, before resuming their separate searches. Occasionally, they found signs of recently occupied villages; once in a while, they caught sight of an Indian or two, but, throughout the long, hot summer, neither Crook nor Terry could engage the elusive enemy.

In mid-August, the summer drought gave way to cold, incessant rains. By the end of the month, there was frost on the ground at night. Supplies were short and tempers were shorter. Marching on half rations, many soldiers had dysentery and scurvy. They were, as Lt. John Bourke said, "wet, cross, hungry, and disgusted." Whenever one of the cavalry horses or pack mules died, it was immediately eaten: "I am a hippophagist," a Colonel Carr wrote home.

On September 8, a scouting party under Capt. Anson Mills caught sight of a Lakota village at the east end of a ridge in northwestern South Dakota called Slim Buttes. Sending word to Crook to join him, Mills led his 100 men in a surprise attack on the village. After some initial resistance, the Lakota, led by Oglala Lakota chief American Horse, withdrew before Mills himself suffered a surprise attack when Crazy Horse led out his warriors at the gallop from a nearby but unnoticed Lakota village. Crazy Horse attacked and withdrew, suffering only light casualties.

When the fighting was done, Mills and Crook had burnt some 37 tipis at Slim Buttes. It was not only the army's only victory but its only engagement since the Battle of the Little Bighorn. The discovery of horses and saddles that had belonged to Custer's Seventh Cavalry brought the fight at Slim Buttes greater nationwide publicity than its military significance warranted.

After Slim Buttes, Crook and his men withdrew to Fort Fetterman to sit out the winter. Yet it was during that winter that the U.S. Army had its first truly significant engagement since Little Bighorn. In early November, Crook got word of a Cheyenne village in the Big Horn Mountains called Dull Knife, after the Cheyenne chief. Despite the harsh winter weather, Crook ordered Col. Ranald Mackenzie, accompanied by an enormous force of 11 cavalry, 11 infantry, four artillery companies, and some 400 Indian scouts—2,000 men in all—to scout out the village. Crook himself followed after Mackenzie.

On November 25, Mackenzie located Dull Knife, a village of some 183 tipis, which he attacked and destroyed early in the morning of November 26. By the time Crook arrived, the fighting was over and the few Indian survivors had fled. Again, the soldiers found many items captured from Custer's men at Little Bighorn, including a roster book, later used to help establish who had died with Custer. After separating out food supplies, which they sorely needed, Crook's men torched the village.

The Battle of Dull Knife was the beginning of the end for the Northern Cheyenne. Virtually the entire tribe not then living on reservations had been camped at Dull Knife. Most of those who survived the battle soon froze to death as they fled, without horses or food, into the mountains. A few eventually found their way to Crazy Horse's new camp on the Powder River and lived among the Lakota for a number of months.

In April of 1877, these Cheyenne survivors made their way to Fort Robinson (sometimes called Camp Robinson) in northwest Nebraska and surrendered. In May, they were sent to the Cheyenne and Arapaho Agency, an Indian reservation in Oklahoma, where many succumbed to malaria. In 1878, led by Chiefs Little Wolf and Dull Knife, most of the remaining Cheyenne attempted to return to their homeland, but they were rounded up and sent to several reservations.

On January 9, 1879, in what is called the Fort Robinson Uprising, Chief Dull Knife and some 150 Cheyenne held in the Nebraska fort once more decided to return home. That evening, the war chief Little Wolf urged the Cheyenne warriors to "dress up and put on your best

Dull Knife, who was
the war chief of
Northern Cheyenne
at Battle of
Little Bighorn
(National Archives)

clothing. We will all die together." As the men, women, and children fled the fort under cover of darkness, 64 Indians were killed. Soon, another 58 were captured and sent to the Pine Ridge Agency across the border in South Dakota. Only a handful of Cheyenne escaped. No soldiers were killed in the incident, the last serious attempt by the Northern Cheyenne to live freely on the great plains.

While the Cheyenne were being dispatched in the Battle of Dull Knife and its aftermath, the Lakota were having their own troubles. After

Dull Knife in 1876, the talented tactician and energetic campaigner Gen. Nelson Miles set out into the Powder River country in pursuit of Chief Sitting Bull. According to what some historians say is a true story—and what others deem mere legend—Miles and Sitting Bull met face to face under a flag of truce in mid-October 1876. Miles later wrote that he found Sitting Bull "cold, but dignified and courteous." When Miles ordered Sitting Bull to return to the Great Sioux Reservation in Dakota, Sitting Bull insisted in return that the whites leave the Black Hills. Remarking that "God made me an Indian, but not a reservation Indian," Sitting Bull and his party rode off to where the rest of the Lakota warriors waited.

At that point, Miles attacked so quickly that he was later accused (at least by the Lakota) of violating Sitting Bull's flag of truce. After a two-day battle, the army was victorious; within a week, some 2,600 Lakota under Chief White Bull surrendered. As for Sitting Bull himself, he escaped with some of his people to Canada, which the Lakota called "Grandmother's Land."

Miles next turned his attention to tracking down Oglala Lakota chief Crazy Horse, rumored to be somewhere in the Yellowstone Valley. On January 7, 1877, Miles found Crazy Horse's village, which he attacked, killing several warriors and destroying much of the village, although Crazy Horse and many of his people escaped. Now, however, Crazy Horse was on the run, in the dead of a particularly vicious winter, having lost many of his horses and virtually all of his supplies. In May, responding to a message from General Crook that he could live on a reservation in the Powder River country, Crazy Horse led his remaining 800 warriors, splendid in their war regalia, to Fort Robinson, Nebraska, where he surrendered.

It soon became obvious that Crook was not going to be able to persuade his superiors to let Crazy Horse settle in his beloved Powder River country. On September 5, after a series of misunderstandings with Crook, Crazy Horse was placed under arrest. As the great chief realized that he was being shepherded toward the stockade, he drew a knife from beneath his robes, was stabbed by a soldier, and died a few hours later. Like Custer—36 when he made his famous last stand—Crazy Horse, perhaps 35 at the time of his death, died young.

A month to the day after Crazy Horse's death, deep in the Bear Paw Mountains of northern Montana, Chief Joseph and some 5,000 Nez Perce Indians surrendered to the U.S. Army which had tracked them

1,300 miles from their original homeland in Oregon and Idaho to within 30 miles of their intended sanctuary in Canada. Ironically, the Nez Perce were one of the few Indian tribes to have lived in almost complete harmony with the whites, from the days that tribal members assisted Lewis and Clark when their expedition reached Nez Perce territory in 1805 until the early 1860s. Then, treaties hastily enacted at the time of the Oregon gold rush led to a reduction of the Oregon Nez Perce tribal lands from 10,000 to 1,000 acres, all in Idaho. The Nez Perce resisted leaving Oregon, but in May of 1877, Gen. Oliver Howard ordered the Nez Perce to relocate on the Lapwai reservation in Idaho within 30 days.

While the Nez Perce were trying to decide what to do, a minor incident with settlers escalated to bloodshed and the Nez Perce killed some 15 settlers. Chief Joseph, although committed to peace, decided to lead his people on a long journey, in the hope of finding a new homeland to the northeast in Canada. The Nez Perce trekked along the Salmon River, through the Bitterroot Mountains along the Idaho-Montana border, before reaching Montana on July 25. Behind them came General Howard and some 600 soldiers, with whom the Nez Perce fought a number of skirmishes, including a major encounter on August 9 at Big Hole in which at least 89 Indians were killed. Despite this defeat, the Nez Perce made their way into the newly established Yellowstone National Park—to the considerable surprise of a handful of tourists visiting there. In early September, while Howard's troops and reinforcements were guarding the obvious passes out of Yellowstone, the Nez Perce slipped through an obscure and tortuous pass into Montana.

For the next two weeks, the Nez Perce made their way through Montana toward the Canadian border. Exhausted by their trek, they camped by Snake Creek in the Bear Paw Mountains—where they were spotted by one of General Howard's scouts. Howard immediately telegraphed to Gen. Nelson Miles at Fort Keogh on the Yellowstone to join in the chase. On September 30, Miles located Chief Joseph's camp and mounted a successful attack, which effectively destroyed the camp and forced the Nez Perce to flee into the mountains. It was already winter in the mountains, and many who took refuge there froze to death in the bitter cold.

On October 5, General Howard arrived with his troops. Chief Joseph, by then leading only some 350 women and children and 80 men, dictated his famous surrender to a translator, who conveyed it to General Howard. "Tell General Howard I know his heart," Chief Joseph

Chief Joseph, of the Nez Perce, surrendered to General Howard in 1877. *(National Archives)*

said. "What he told me before, I have in my heart. I am tired of fighting. Our chiefs are killed . . . The little children are freezing to death. My people, some of them, have run away to the hills, and have no blankets, no food. No one knows where they are—perhaps freezing to death. I want to have time to look for my children and see how many I can find. Maybe I shall find them among the dead. Hear me, my chiefs. I am tired. My heart is sick and sad. From where the sun now stands, I will fight no more forever."

Although General Howard had promised Chief Joseph that he could return to a reservation in Oregon if he surrendered, the chief was first sent south to a Kansas reservation before being dispatched to the Colville Reservation in Washington, where he would die in 1904. Lt. Charles Erskine Wood, an aide to General Howard, later wrote of Chief Joseph that "in his long career, Joseph cannot accuse the United States of one single act of justice."

By 1879, the army had made substantial progress in its campaign to deal a final blow to the great Plains Indians tribes, the Cheyenne and the Sioux. In addition, the army had dealt effectively with several lesser tribes, including the Shoshone, Paiute, and Bannock (or Bannack), who had once ranged from Kansas into the Pacific Northwest. Then, an incident on a reservation in Colorado occurred involving the Ute Indians, whose homeland had once included much of Utah. During the Black Hawk War of 1865–68, the Ute under Chief Ouray had harassed Mormon settlers in Utah. After they surrendered in 1868, the Ute had been relocated in Colorado.

There matters rested until about 1876, when Colorado became a state and new settlers cast covetous eyes on the Ute reservation land. The slogan "Utes Must Go!" became a popular one. In September of 1879, Nathan Meeker, an Indian agent detested by the Ute for his avarice and cruelty, asked for protection from federal troops. When they got word that the soldiers were coming, the Ute warriors rode out to meet them at Milk Creek, on the outskirts of the reservation. Shots were fired—once again, no one seems to know who fired first—and the Ute and soldiers fought on and off for the next week. During this time, some Ute warriors killed Meeker and nine other agency workers.

When the fighting died down and the outnumbered Ute surrendered, Colorado governor Frederick Pitkin immediately appropriated the Ute reservation and opened it to settlement. Most of the Ute were moved out of Colorado and sent to a small, barren reservation in Utah, although Chief Ouray and his tribe were allowed to settle on a reservation in southwest Colorado.

By 1880, the army command was feeling justifiably proud of its success after the debacle at Little Bighorn. Yet it rankled that Sitting Bull, one of the leaders of the Lakota assault on Custer, was living a free life in Canada. Furthermore, there was real concern that at any time Sitting Bull might lead his remaining warriors back into the United States and try to resume his life on the plains. In 1881, General Terry led a delegation to Fort Buford, Canada, to persuade Sitting Bull to return home. For various reasons, including pressure from Canadian authorities, Sitting Bull agreed. On July 29, he and about 200 other Lakota boarded the steamship *General Sherman* and headed down the Missouri to Fort Yates. From there, he was sent, in direct violation of U.S. promises, to Fort Randall, South Dakota. Two years later, Sitting Bull was moved to the Standing Rock Reservation in North Dakota, where

FROM LITTLE BIGHORN TO THE GHOST DANCE

Buffalo Bill Cody, although he could be friendly with Indians in some situations, was also a scout for the army in pursuit of Indians. He is shown here (on white horse, left) apparently advising Gen. Nelson Miles (on black horse, center). *(Library of Congress)*

agent James McLaughlin handed him a hoe and urged him to till the soil. Small wonder that Sitting Bull leapt at the opportunity in 1885 to tour America and Europe in Buffalo Bill's famous Wild West Show.

At about the same time that Sitting Bull was making his first appearances with Buffalo Bill, another Indian chief captured the nation's attention: Geronimo (Goyathlay), the leader of the Chiricahua Apache. In 1885, Geronimo and about 50 Chiricahua Apache fled their Arizona reservation and attempted to resume their former nomadic life on the southern plains. When the U.S. Army learned that Geronimo was on the loose, they took it seriously. In 1880, Geronimo and another Apache chief, Victorio, had mounted a number of raids on settlers in Arizona, New Mexico, and Texas. After Victorio's death in 1880, Geronimo had led several hundred Apache into hiding in Mexico. For the next few years, Geronimo's band had raided settlements across the border in the United States, where the lighting speed of their attacks made them greatly feared.

Between 1882 and 1884, Geronimo and the experienced Indian fighter General Crook had played a cat-and-mouse game back and forth across the Mexican border. In 1884, Crook had managed to persuade most of the Apache, including Geronimo, to return to their Arizona reservation at San Carlos. "For the first time in the history of that fierce people," Crook wrote, "every member of the Apache tribe is at peace." The peace was brief. On May 17, 1885, Geronimo and about 150

Apache again slipped off the reservation and headed for the border with Mexico, with General Crook soon in pursuit. The next year, in something of a comedy of errors, Crook first captured, then lost, Geronimo and his band. General Sheridan, Crook's superior, was furious, and replaced Crook with General Miles.

Buffalo Bill and His Wild West Show

BEFORE HE ENTERED SHOW BUSINESS, BUFFALO BILL (William Cody) prospected for gold in California, rode with the Pony Express, and was a superb army scout and marksman, tracking the movements of "hostiles," as the soldiers called the Indians. He earned his nickname from killing buffalo to supply meat to the railroad crews. It was Buffalo Bill's boast that he personally had shot 4,200 buffalo. In 1869, Buffalo Bill was catapulted to fame by Ned Buntline's novel *Buffalo Bill, King of the Border Men;* three years later, Buntline wrote his first play, *The Scouts of the Plain,* and persuaded Buffalo Bill himself to be the star. In the 1870s, Buffalo Bill, along with another western hero, the cowboy known as Texas Jack, and the exotic singer Mademoiselle Giuseppina Morlacchi, spent winters touring and appearing on stage. Each summer, Buffalo Bill returned to the West, where he worked as an army scout. In 1882, Buffalo Bill organized a massive Fourth of July celebration at his farm in Kansas. The show reenacted buffalo hunts, horse roundups, Pony Express rides, and Indian battles, including Custer's Last Stand. The "Old Glory Blowout" was such a success that Buffalo Bill took it on the road as "Buffalo Bill's Wild West Show." In 1885, Buffalo Bill scored his greatest stage coup: Sitting Bull—popularly believed to have been critical in the defeat and death of Gen. George Custer at Little Bighorn—joined the Wild West Show, along with the superb horsewoman and sharpshooter Annie Oakley. Sitting Bull sold his autograph to countless little boys, gave most of the money away, developed an affection for good cigars and oyster stew, and was proud of his handsome white horse, a gift from Buffalo Bill. When Sitting Bull was killed in 1890, his horse mistook the fray for an episode from the Wild West Show, and began to prance about in his usual routine. When Buffalo Bill got word of Sitting Bull's death, he bought back the horse that had so often performed with them both.

In this photograph, taken on March 26, 1886, General Crook is shown negotiating with the Apache warrior Geronimo (center, facing) to persuade him to surrender. *(National Archives)*

For the next five months, Miles and some 5,000 U.S. Army troops pursued Geronimo and his band of some 24 warriors across Arizona and New Mexico. Finally, in the summer of 1886, Geronimo surrendered to Miles. Most of the Apache with Geronimo, and many who had remained on the reservation, were resettled first at Fort Marion, Florida, and then in Alabama and at Fort Sill, Oklahoma, far from their homeland. Thus ended what the official U.S. government report issued in 1886 described as Geronimo's "career of murder and robbery unparalleled in the history of Indian raids." In his autobiography, which he dictated in 1905–06, Geronimo put it differently: "The Indians," he said, "always tried to live peaceably with the white soldiers and settlers," but after broken treaties and unkept promises, "the Indians agreed not to be friendly with the white men any more" and "a long struggle followed."

With Sitting Bull now a "rodeo Indian" and Geronimo in captivity, by 1886 the long struggle of the Plains Indians was coming to an end. The Indians of both the northern and southern plains were defeated and leaderless. In addition, tribal hopes for future leaders had been substantially diminished by the creation of distant off-reservation boarding schools for young Indians. Of these, the best known was the Carlisle School in Pennsylvania, founded in 1879, where all the school-age children in Geronimo's tribe were sent after his defeat.

Carlisle's founder, Capt. Richard Pratt, was considered a liberal and a humanitarian for believing that Indian youth could benefit from a good education and vocational training. Not only were the children educated in the "white man's ways," every sign of their own culture was systematically eradicated: Children who arrived in traditional costume were immediately put into uniforms. Speaking anything but English was prohibited by teachers who were determined to wipe out "savage ways." Even teachers like Elaine Goodale Eastman, who chose to teach on the Great Sioux Reservation in the 1880s, and who revealed her sympathies by calling her memoirs *Sister to the Sioux,* found it necessary to title one chapter of her memoirs "Indians are People!". Anglo-Americans, even those who supported Native Americans, could not accept Indians, whose lifestyles and customs were simply too different from theirs, as equals.

During the years after Little Bighorn when the U.S. Army was fighting and rounding up the last free Indians on the Great Plains, a flood of

This group of Apache prisoners seated on the embankment—including Geronimo, third from right in front row—is being taken by federal troops to prison in Florida in 1886. *(National Archives)*

FROM LITTLE BIGHORN TO THE GHOST DANCE

People are depicted here on horseback and in wagons racing for land claims in Oklahoma. *(Library of Congress, Prints & Photographs Division [LC-USZ62-77823])*

legislation from Washington accelerated the region's settlement by whites. By 1884, virtually all of the Dakota Territory was opened for settlement, and in 1887 the Dawes Allotment Act put an effective end to reservations held in communal tribal ownership. Under the terms of the act, each family would receive 160 acres to farm. The remaining land—some 86 million acres, fully 62 percent of the land set aside for the Plains Indians—was opened to homesteaders. Ironically, the act was strongly supported by reformers who thought that the Indians were demeaned by reservation life and would do better as farmers.

On one day alone—February 23, 1889—President Grover Cleveland signed legislation allowing North and South Dakota, Montana, and Washington to enter the Union as states, which they did in the autumn of that year, followed in 1890 by Idaho and Wyoming. On April 22, 1889, the former Indian territory of Oklahoma was opened to settlement: 1,920,000 acres were made available. So many homesteaders streamed across the border that Oklahoma City was populated by 10,000 squatters by nightfall. Then, on February 11, 1890, President

Benjamin Harrison signed legislation opening half of the 22 million acres of the Great Sioux Reservation in Dakota to settlement.

By 1890, the series of military victories after Little Bighorn, along with sweeping government legislation, seemed to have put an end to the long struggle of the Plains Indians to maintain their traditional life on the Great Plains. But just when the Indians' struggle seemed over, hopes rose again, thanks to the teachings of the mystic leader called Wovoka and the visionary movement he founded, called the Ghost Dance.

9

WOUNDED KNEE
AND AFTER

By 1890, successful military campaigns and legislation such as the Dawes Allotment Act of 1887 had effectively destroyed life on the plains for the Indians. A final blow seemed to come on February 11, 1890, when President Benjamin Harrison signed legislation opening half of the remaining 22 million acres of the Great Sioux Reservation to settlement. Then, a religious movement called the Ghost Dance swept across the plains, uniting many of the Plains Indians in one last attempt to reclaim their homeland and resume their traditional way of life.

Like most great religious movements, the Ghost Dance originated in the visions and teachings of a charismatic leader. In this case, the leader was Wovoka, or Wanekia, whose name is sometimes translated "Cutter." A member of the Northern Paiute (Numu) tribe, Wovoka was born around 1858 in the Walker River country of Mason Valley, Nevada, some 50 miles southeast of the present-day city of Reno. Wovoka's father, a medicine man and mystic named Tavibo, died when Wovoka was a boy, and the youth was raised by white neighbors, the Wilsons, who were devout Christians. From boyhood, Wovoka, who also went by the name Jack Wilson, was exposed both to traditional Indian religious beliefs and to Christianity.

On January 1, 1889, during a solar eclipse, Wovoka, then in his early thirties, had the first of a number of visions that combined aspects of his two religious traditions. In his vision, Wovoka saw all the buffalo and all the Indians who had ever lived returning to live again on the plains, led by a Christlike messiah. All this would be brought about, Wovoka's vision revealed, by performing a special dance called the Ghost Dance. The Ghost Dance's combination of traditional Indian mysticism and Christianity made it appeal both to those Indians who had accepted Christianity and to those who had maintained their original religious beliefs. In addition, many of those who took up the Ghost Dance would enter into religious trances in which beatific visions were not uncommon.

News of Wovoka's vision quickly spread among the Paiute Indians, and from them across the plains to other tribes, often carried by Indians traveling on the trains that now criss-crossed former Indian territory. Wovoka's message was irresistible: He preached the return of the buffalo and long-dead loved ones, and the disappearance of the hated white soldiers and settlers. Once-powerful tribes such as the Arapaho, Cheyenne, and Lakota sent delegates to Wovoka at the Paiute Reservation in Walker Lake, Nevada, to learn how to do the Ghost Dance. By 1890, white authorities were increasingly concerned about the movement. The dance itself reminded whites all too much of Indian war dances, and Wovoka's preachings about the return of the good old days alarmed the settlers who had fought to win the West. Matters began to come to a head in March of 1890, when a Lakota delegation that had visited Wovoka returned to the Pine Ridge Agency, one of the five Sioux reservations in the Dakotas.

The Lakota delegation told their tribespeople that Wovoka had revealed that he himself was the promised messiah. In addition, Wovoka had suggested that the whites would soon disappear in punishment for their wickedness. Wovoka's vision had been peaceful and vague as to the details of precisely how the whites would disappear. However, many Lakota interpreted Wovoka's vision to mean that they would now defeat the whites in battle as they had previously been defeated. The Lakota hopes of victory were increased by their belief that any Indian who wore a special Ghost Shirt—a long, loose white cotton or muslin garment—would be protected against the bullets of the whites. This belief was quite contrary to Wovoka's own vision of the Ghost Shirt as a sacred garment, not as a magical suit of armor.

The Lakota who had visited Wovoka also brought back tales of the miracles they had experienced, in which they had talked with long-dead relatives and seen dead buffalo brought back to life. The visions of plenty seemed to be an answer to one of the prayers sung by Ghost Dancers:

Dear Father, have pity on me,
I have nothing to eat;
I am dying of thirst,
everything I had is gone.

Jack Red Cloud, son of the great chief Red Cloud who had forced the government to close the Bozeman Trail in 1868, was one of the first Lakota to embrace the Ghost Dance religion, although his father was noncommittal about the new religion. Soon, many of the 6,000 Oglala Lakota at Pine Ridge were dancing the Ghost Dance day and night. Articles on the dance soon appeared in popular eastern publications such as *Harper's Weekly* and *Frank Leslie's Illustrated Newspaper*. In her memoirs, *Sister to the Sioux,* teacher Elaine Goodale Eastman later wrote sympathetically of a dance she saw at Pine Ridge:

Under the soft glow of the hunter's moon perhaps a hundred men, women, and children, with clasped hands and fingers interlocked, swung in a great circle about their 'sacred tree,' chanting together the monotonous Ghost Dance songs. The hypnotic repetition of the words: "Once more we shall hunt the buffalo—Our Father has said it!" alternated with short invocations by prophet or priest and occasional intervals of wailing by the women—that musical heart-piercing sound which, once heard, is never forgotten. No one with imagination could fail to see in the rite a genuine religious ceremony, a faith which, illusory as it was, deserved to be treated with respect.

Eastman's enlightened view of the Ghost Dance was hardly typical. Across the plains there was growing concern about the Ghost Dance among settlers, Indian agents, and the military. On November 15, 1890, Pine Ridge Indian agent D. F. Royer sent a telegram to Washington asking for troops, reporting that "Indians are dancing in the snow and are wild and crazy . . . We need protection."

Royer's message was relayed to General Miles, commander of the Division of the Missouri, at his Chicago headquarters. Miles took what Royer had to say seriously, believing, as he later said, that the Lakota were "far better prepared to wage war than at any previous time in history." Miles based his belief on his knowledge that many of the reservation Lakota had armed themselves with the deadly rapid-fire Winchester rifles.

This picture of Arapaho Indians performing the Ghost Dance conveys the communal and ceremonial nature of the dance. *(National Archives)*

On November 20, the first troops, including the African-American Buffalo Soldiers of the Ninth and Tenth Cavalry, began to arrive at the Pine Ridge and Rosebud Agencies. Almost at once, many Indians, rightly suspecting that the soldiers would forbid the Ghost Dance, began to slip away from the agency. By the end of the month, as many as 3,000 Lakota had left the reservations to live in the nearby hills known as the Badlands. Journalists, who rushed to Pine Ridge to cover the anticipated hostilities, wired alarmist accounts of the Ghost Dance movement to their newspapers.

In early December, General Miles ordered Col. William Drum, the commanding officer at Fort Yates, North Dakota, to put a stop to ongoing Ghost Dance activity at the nearby Standing Rock Reservation by arresting the influential Lakota leader Chief Sitting Bull. On December 14, the authorities at Fort Yates got word that Sitting Bull was planning to leave Standing Rock to go to Pine Ridge, where many Lakota expected the messiah to appear imminently. The thought of the explosive combination of Sitting Bull and most of the Lakota coming together in one place to await the appearance of a messiah who had promised to rid the land of whites made Colonel Drum act: 43 Indian police, Indians who policed fellow Indians, followed by two troops of cavalry, galloped the 30 miles from Fort Yates to Standing Rock to arrest

Sitting Bull. At dawn on December 15, the Indian police awakened Sitting Bull, and when he called out to his people to protect him, a scuffle broke out. When it was over, Sitting Bull lay dead, along with eight of his warriors and six of the Indian police.

With Sitting Bull dead, the army turned its attention to Chiefs Hump and Big Foot, both Miniconjou had been active in the Ghost Dance movement. Hump surrendered almost immediately; when the Eighth Cavalry under Lt. Col. E. V. Sumner caught up with Big Foot and his Miniconjou Lakota band not far from the Standing Rock Reservation, Big Foot promised to return to the reservation, but slipped away at night. On December 28, as the Eighth Cavalry continued to round up small bands of Lakota, some 200 soldiers from Custer's old regiment, the Seventh Cavalry, came upon Big Foot and some 340 Lakota in the Porcupine Creek valley in Pine Ridge Reservation territory.

Big Foot had been trying to lead his people, many women and children, to what he felt would be a safer place with Chief Red Cloud's band. The weather was bitter cold, and he had pneumonia, was coughing blood, and could travel only stretched out on a travois. After

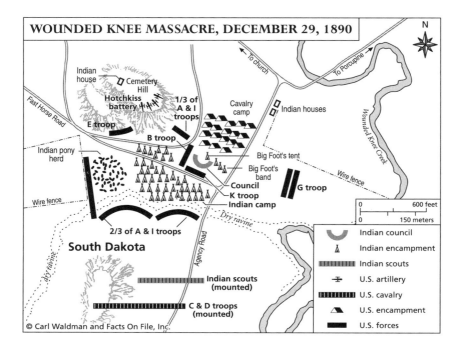

WOUNDED KNEE MASSACRE, DECEMBER 29, 1890

negotiations with the Seventh Cavalry's Maj. S. M. Whitside, Big Foot agreed to an unconditional surrender. Big Foot was placed on an army ambulance wagon and the Indians, escorted by the Seventh Cavalry, proceeded to Wounded Knee Creek, which rises in southwest South Dakota and flows northwest to the White River. Accompanying the Seventh Cavalry was a party of journalists, including the artist Frederic Remington, on assignment to do sketches of any action for *Harper's Weekly.*

Major Whitside's squadron was soon joined by the main body of the Seventh Cavalry, some 438 cavalrymen led by Col. George Forsyth. Forsyth's orders were to camp for the night by the reservation store and post office at Wounded Knee Creek before marching the Indians to the Union Pacific railroad station at Gordon, Nebraska. From Gordon, Big Foot's band was to be sent by train to the military prison at Omaha, Nebraska. General Miles's orders to Forsyth said that he should "use force enough" to accomplish this.

Members of the U.S. Indian Police, divisions that patrolled reservations
(National Archives)

A photograph of the Indian encampment at Pine Ridge reservation, South Dakota, a few weeks before the massacre at nearby Wounded Knee Creek. *(Library of Congress)*

At Wounded Knee, the soldiers set up their four rapid-fire Hotch-kiss guns on a hill overlooking the Indian camp, where Big Foot's tipi flew a white flag. That night, the soldiers broke out a barrel of whiskey to celebrate capturing Big Foot. In the morning, after deploying his men so that Big Foot's camp was surrounded, Forsyth ordered the Lakota warriors to hand over their firearms. When only a few aged and rusty firearms were produced, Forsyth became suspicious and ordered his men to search the tipis for the modern Winchester rifles he believed Big Foot's warriors had. As the soldiers rummaged through the tipis, tempers began to rise. According to one version, the medicine man Yellow Bird started to dance the Ghost Dance and sang a song reminding the Sioux that their Ghost Shirts would protect them against any bullets.

No one knows precisely what happened next. Shots rang out; no one knows who fired first, although eyewitnesses on both sides said it was Black Coyote, a young Sioux determined not to surrender his Winches-ter rifle. What is known is that when the firing stopped, Big Foot and most of his band had been shot and killed. Estimates of the dead range from as few as 146 to as many as 300. The dead bodies of women and children who fled when the fighting began were later found as far as three miles away from the camp. Louise Weasel Bear, who survived the battle, later said, "We tried to run, but they shot us like we were a buf-falo." Twenty-five members of the Seventh Cavalry were killed, many caught in the crossfire of the Hotchkiss guns.

Big Foot, Miniconjou Lakota Sioux chief, a leader of the Indians who were encamped near Wounded Knee Creek, was among those killed on December 29, 1890. His frozen body was found after the massacre. *(Library of Congress)*

Newspaperman William Kelly of the *Nebraska State Journal* got the story of Wounded Knee out by courier to the nearest telegraph office and his scoop ran coast to coast on December 30. Almost immediately, opinion was divided as to whether Wounded Knee was a great victory or a great disgrace. In some accounts, the Indians were portrayed as cunning savages outwitted by the Seventh Cavalry. Others portrayed the Indians as innocent victims of the Seventh Cavalry's long-standing wish to avenge its defeat 14 years earlier at the Battle of Little Bighorn. According to historian George Metcalf, an officer of the Seventh Cavalry was heard to boast "with much gluttonous satisfaction in his voice, 'Now we have avenged Custer's death.'" Elaine Goodale, who had heard the gunfire from Wounded Knee at her home 18 miles away on the Pine Ridge Agency, wrote her own account of that day for the newspapers entitled "Miss Goodale Blames the Troops for the Killing of the Women and the Children." While not blaming Wounded Knee on the Seventh Cavalry's need for revenge, she described what happened as a "general and indiscriminate slaughter of the unarmed and the helpless."

The Indians who died at Wounded Knee were buried there in a common grave on New Year's Day, 1891. Doctor Charles Eastman, the future husband of Elaine Goodale, and himself a Dakota Sioux, accompanied the burial detail from the Pine Ridge Reservation to the battlefield to search for survivors. Eastman later wrote in his autobiography that the scene of carnage at Wounded Knee was "a severe ordeal for one who had so lately put all his faith in the Christian love and lofty ideals of the white man." Among the frozen corpses, Eastman found a handful of survivors: five adults, two children, and a four-month-old baby girl who was later adopted by Brig. Gen. L. W. Colby of the Nebraska militia.

Between January 14 and 16, 1891, just two weeks after Wounded Knee, the last Sioux still living off the reservations surrendered in small groups wherever they were captured to General Miles. Within months,

These Lakota Sioux chiefs met with General Miles and helped negotiate the end of the Plains Indian Wars. Shown are Standing Bull, Bear Who Looks Back Running (Stands and Looks Back), Has the Big White Horse, White Tail, Liver (Living) Bear, Little Thunder, Bull Dog, High Hawk, Lame, and Eagle Pipe. *(Library of Congress, Prints & Photographs Division [LC-DIG-ppmsc-02514])*

the Ghost Dance had been abandoned. General Miles himself was almost immediately suspicious that Wounded Knee had been more of a massacre than a battle and influenced President Harrison to order an inquiry "as to killing of women and children at Wounded Knee Creek." The final report concluded that "There is nothing to conceal or apologize for in the Wounded Knee Battle . . . The firing was begun by the Indians and continued until they stopped." Subsequently, three officers and 15 enlisted men were awarded the Medal of Honor for heroism at Wounded Knee. General Miles protested every inch of the way at what he considered to be the whitewash of Wounded Knee; as late as 1920, when he was 81, he urged Congress to compensate the relatives of the Lakota who died there.

The Baby Who Survived Wounded Knee

ON NEW YEAR'S DAY 1891, THREE DAYS AFTER THE December 29, 1890, massacre at Wounded Knee, Dr. Charles Eastman set out from the Pine Ridge Reservation to gather the dead for burial on the battlefield and search for any survivors (a snowstorm had prevented their going earlier). Eastman and his party were about to head back when someone heard a baby's faint cry from under her mother's frozen corpse. The infant—not yet a year old—was rushed back to Pine Ridge, where a wet nurse coaxed her to feed. Word of the child, quickly named the "Lost Bird of Wounded Knee," spread, and competition was fierce to lay claim to the "miracle infant." Buffalo Bill's agent wanted to raise the infant for future appearance in sideshows, but the child went to handsome, dashing general Leonard Colby, whose wife, Clara, was an early feminist and suffragist. It seemed to be a happy ending but was not. The Colby marriage was unhappy and when the marriage failed, Lost Bird, known by her Lakota name of Zintka, was viewed as a burden by both her adoptive parents. As she grew up, she encountered racial prejudice, and, not surprisingly, had serious emotional difficulties. Ironically, as an adult, Zintka appeared in circuses and sideshows, before dying young, of syphilis. In 1991, her body was exhumed from her grave in California and buried by the common grave of those who fell at Wounded Knee.

Showing the disregard for Indian life prevalent at the time, part of the caption that accompanied this photograph of members of the military who fought at Wounded Knee reads, "These brave men and the Hotchkiss gun that Big Foot's Indians thought were toys, together with the fighting 7th what's left of Gen. Custer's boys, sent 200 Indians to that Heaven which the ghost dancer enjoys." *(Library of Congress, Prints & Photographs Division [LC-USZ62-11974])*

Anthropologist James Mooney also investigated the Ghost Dance movement and Wounded Knee for the Bureau of Indian Affairs. Mooney's detailed and sensitive *The Ghost Dance Religion and the Sioux Outbreak of 1890,* published by the Bureau of American Ethnology in 1896, is a landmark in Indian studies. Today most historians of the Plains Indian Wars view Wounded Knee, along with Sand Creek (1864), as more massacre than battle, although some, such as historian Robert M. Utley, regard Wounded Knee simply as a "tragic accident of war."

After Wounded Knee, despite minor cavalry skirmishes with the Cheyenne in 1894 and the Bannock in 1895, and the brief uprising of the Oklahoma Creek Indians in 1901, real warfare on the plains was at an end. Appropriately, it was also in 1890 that the Bureau of the Census declared that coast-to-coast settlement meant that "there can hardly be said to be a frontier line." The Indians, who had tried to hold back the frontier for so long, had failed, and America had realized its Manifest Destiny to settle all the land that lay between the Atlantic and the Pacific.

In a soon-to-be-famous address to the American Historical Society in 1893, Frederick Jackson Turner spoke of the significance of the frontier in American society. More than any other factor, Turner speculated, the existence of the frontier explained American social development. The frontier, Turner suggested, was the "meeting point between savagery and civilization." In addition, Turner posited, the "Indian frontier" had been the great "consolidating agent" in American history, a "common danger, demanding united action."

In short, Turner concluded that the frontier's repeated demands for unity, renewal, and progress had formed the American character. At the same time, the powerful combination of military force, westward settlement, and legislative action that had driven the frontier to the Pacific had put an end to virtually every aspect of the traditional way of life of the Plains Indians. It would take much of the 20th century before the Plains Indians were able to make substantial strides to reclaim a heritage all but lost in the Plains Indian Wars.

10

HISTORY AND MYTH

In retrospect, it is clear that the Plains Indian Wars ended when the last of the Lakota surrendered to General Miles after Wounded Knee in January 1891. At the time, of course, no one could have known this; in fact, throughout 1891 rumors of a resurgence of the Ghost Dance movement made both settlers and soldiers edgy. Newspapers and magazines reported that the campaign against the Ghost Dancing Sioux, not the Plains Indian Wars, had ended. The correspondent for *Harper's Weekly* recorded that Miles held a great review of his troops to mark the occasion—but not even Miles could have known that this would be the last time that his troops would celebrate a victory over the Indians by marching to the strains of Custer's favorite march, "Gerry Owen."

The surrender of the Lakota in January 1891 ended what remains to this day the longest campaign ever fought by the U.S. Army. Between 1865 and 1891, the U.S. Army and the Plains Indians exchanged fire in more than 1,000 incidents. Civilian casualties on both sides are impossible to estimate, in part because contemporary newspaper reports tended to exaggerate both victories and defeats. The official U.S. Army casualty figures were 1,944. There is no accurate record of the number of Indian warriors who died during the Plains Indian Wars, in part because the Indians almost never left their dead on the battlefield. Most historians, however, believe that if one takes into account civilian casualties, far more Indians than settlers died in the war.

By the end of the decade that had begun with Wounded Knee, legislation had stripped the Plains Indians of much of their remaining land. As a Lakota living on the Pine Ridge Reservation put it after Wounded Knee, the whites "made us many promises, more than I can

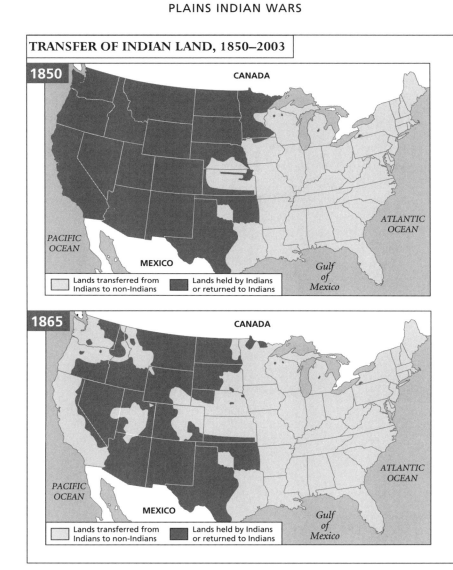

TRANSFER OF INDIAN LAND, 1850–2003

remember, but they never kept but one; they promised to take our land and they took it."

In 1891, President Benjamin Harrison opened 900,000 acres of Indian land in Oklahoma to settlement, followed by 3 million more Oklahoma acres the next year. On September 16, 1893, Harrison's

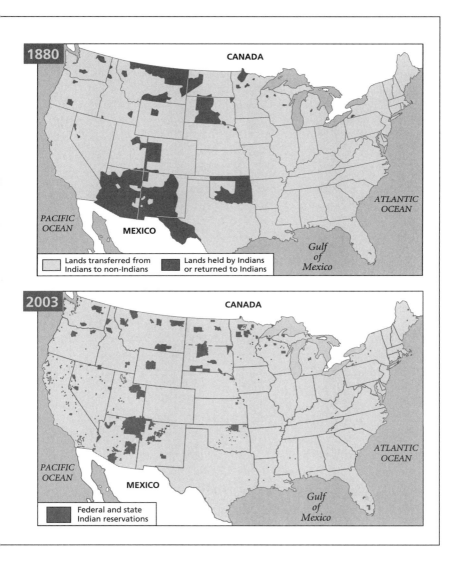

1880

CANADA

ATLANTIC
OCEAN

PACIFIC
OCEAN

MEXICO

Lands transferred from
Indians to non-Indians

Lands held by Indians
or returned to Indians

Gulf
of
Mexico

2003

CANADA

ATLANTIC
OCEAN

PACIFIC
OCEAN

MEXICO

Federal and state
Indian reservations

Gulf
of
Mexico

successor, President Grover Cleveland, opened a staggering 6,500,000 acres of Oklahoma's Cherokee strip to homesteaders. On the first day alone, some 50,000 homesteaders dashed into the Cherokee strip and staked out land claims. With all this activity, the creation of the Dawes Commission the same year to oversee "reorganizing" of tribal land seems almost superfluous. In 1897, the Dawes Commission allotted 40-acre homesteads to families in the Choctaw and Chickasaw Nations before opening the rest of the tribal land to settlers. Finally, in 1898 the Curtis Act authorized the allotment of individual grants to families before opening all remaining tribal land to settlement. The Curtis Act also effectively destroyed tribal government by outlawing tribal institutions.

In short, after losing their wide-ranging life on the plains during the Plains Indian Wars, during the last years of the 19th century and the opening decades of the 20th, the Plains Indians were steadily stripped of their traditional institutions and virtually all of their remaining land. Between the time that oil was discovered in Oklahoma in 1897, and 1914, 27 million of the 30 million acres set aside for Indians in the Oklahoma territory were opened to white settlement. The remaining 3 million acres were alloted to individual Indian families in small parcels of about 160 acres. Within a few generations, repeated inheritance diminished these holdings still further and made profitable farming virtually impossible. This, in turn, led to the widespread unemployment and poverty endemic to this day on most reservations.

The government's policy of assimilation attempted to put an end to the "Indian problem" by repressing every aspect of Native American culture, including languages and religious beliefs. This policy of stamping out "Indianness," which had been implemented on reservations and in Indian schools even before the end of the Plains Indian Wars, was accelerated after open hostilities ceased. Often, well-meaning "reformers" eager to see the Indians take their place in white society supported the very measures that effectively destroyed Indian institutions. All too often the reformers wished only to turn Indians into whites who would farm the land and live in sod or wooden houses. This policy is best symbolized by Indian agent James McLaughlin's handing a hoe to Sitting Bull after his surrender in 1881 and urging him to till the soil. Reservation authorities often simply outlawed living in tipis; standard one-room wood houses were built for many reservation Indians. Chief Flying Hawk, a nephew of Sitting Bull, protested the practice, saying that "The tepee is much better to live in; always clean, warm in winter, cool in summer; easy to move." The point, of course, of the government policy was that the Indians were not to move about but to lead settled lives.

The government also attempted to accelerate assimilation by outlawing central aspects of Indian life in ways that today are viewed by

At schools such as the Carlisle Indian School in Pennsylvania, Indian boys and girls were forced to abandon their native culture and to study subjects such as physics. *(National Archives)*

most Americans as striking examples of cultural genocide. Indian religious practices of central importance, such as the singing of traditional songs and holding tribal feasts, were systematically outlawed. In 1910, both sweat house and Sun Dance ceremonies were forbidden as the government continued its policy to "Christianize and civilize" the Indians. No detail that might promote assimilation was overlooked: Indian boys sent to the Carlisle School had their long hair cut immediately upon arrival, and neither boys nor girls were allowed to speak their native language or wear tribal costumes.

In fact, most whites commonly described as "uncivilized" those Indians who "still wore the blanket." An almost worse insult was to say that someone had "gone back to the blanket," which clearly implied a willful turning away from "civilization." In his autobiography, published in 1933, Chief Luther Standing Bear recalled his days at the Carlisle School in the 1880s and ruminated on these issues. "Many times," he wrote, "we have been laughed at for our native way of dressing, but could anything we ever wore compare in utter foolishness to the steel-ribbed corset and the huge bustle which our girls adopted after a few years in school?"

At the same time that this rigorous suppression of virtually every aspect of Indian life and culture was taking place, many whites began to

In a typical popular play from the end of the 19th century, the Indian is, on the one hand, recognized for what he has become, but the message remains: unless the "red-skin" is "noble," he is a "savage." *(Library of Congress)*

develop a highly romanticized image of the Indian. This image can be traced almost to the first moments of contact between Europeans and Indians. But it was not until the Indians had effectively been destroyed that the image of the "noble savage"—first expressed when Columbus marveled in his journals at the gentle good nature of the Natives peoples he encountered—took on a powerful life of its own. And the Indian most closely identified with the "noble savage" was the Plains Indian—the last to be defeated—especially the Sioux warrior with his flowing headdress.

The painter George Catlin had been one of the first to popularize the image of the Plains Indian as "noble savage." In 1839, Catlin put together a collection of Indian artifacts and some 422 of the paintings that he had done on his trips west of the Mississippi during the 1830s. Catlin called his collection "Catlin's Indian Gallery" and took it on tour through the eastern United States in 1839 and 1840. When he could afford them, Catlin hired Indians to don war paint and perform war dances at his exhibitions. When he was short of funds, which he almost always was, Catlin enlisted family members, including a stalwart young nephew, to disguise themselves and perform Indian dances. Catlin's greatest successes came in the 1840s in London, where he entertained Queen Victoria and put on a display of bow-and-arrow shooting at Lord's Cricket Ground. In 1845, Catlin showed his works at the Louvre in Paris, but by the 1850s, both the European and American public had had its fill of Catlin's Indian Gallery. The artist spent his last years trying unsuccessfully to persuade Congress to purchase the Indian Gallery, but many argued that it was unconscionable to spend money to purchase portraits of the very Indians who had killed whites. Catlin died, penniless, in 1872; in 1879, the National Gallery of Art accepted what remained of the Indian Gallery—much had been lost or sold—as a gift from Catlin's heirs.

Catlin was not the only artist to head across the Mississippi in the 1830s to record Indian life on the Great Plains. One of the most unusual was the Swiss watercolorist Karl Bodmer, who traveled with his patron, Prince Alexander Maximilian of Wied Neuwied in Prussia. Like Catlin, Bodmer recorded scenes of Indians living along the Missouri

Karl Bodmer, the visiting Swiss artist, painted (circa 1834) Mandan Indians performing their Buffalo Dance, yet another sign of the close relationship between the Plains Indians and the buffalo. *(National Archives)*

This 1863 painting of the Rocky Mountains by Albert Bierstadt is typical of his style. *(Library of Congress, Prints & Photographs Division [LC-USZ62-24182])*

River Valley, including the Mandan, soon to become virtually extinct after the devastating smallpox epidemic of 1837. Bodmer often worked in trying conditions: sketching in temperatures as low as 46 degrees below zero and painting scenes of the weeklong Assiniboine

siege of Fort MacKenzie in 1833, while Prince Maximilian fought beside the U.S. soldiers.

Perhaps the greatest 19th-century painter of western panoramas was Albert Bierstadt, born in Germany in 1830 but raised in Massachusetts.

Bierstadt's paintings of wagon trains, Indian villages, and the western landscape brought the frontier into the art galleries of the eastern United States. Catlin and Bodmer recorded a way of life soon to be lost, but Bierstadt recorded one that had virtually disappeared altogether, as when he painted one of the last of the free Plains Indian warriors hunting *The Last of the Buffalo* (1888).

The painters who did the most to popularize the image of the Plains Indian were probably two artists who are even better known for their paintings of the cowboy: Frederic Remington and Charles Russell. A prodigious worker, Remington turned out 2,750 paintings and drawings between 1881 and 1909. Although Remington was ultimately best known for his cavalrymen, cowboys, and horses, *Return of a Blackfoot War Party* (1887) was one of his first popular paintings. Like Bierstadt's *Last of the Buffalo*, Remington's *Indian, Horse, and Village* of 1908 shows a vanished way of life, as do Russell's paintings of buffalo hunts.

While painters were familiarizing Americans with images of the Great Plains and the Plains Indians, a torrent of stage plays, Wild West shows, and dime novels were also carrying the image of the "noble savage" from coast to coast. The first of the dime novels, *Malaeska: The Indian Wife of the White Hunter*, appeared in 1860 and was immediately followed by a flood of other western adventure stories. One novelist,

With such paintings as this, *A Dash for the Timer* (1889), showing cowboys pursued by Apache, Frederic Remington was a major contributor to the image of the American West as a struggle between "good" whites and "bad" Indians. *(Library of Congress)*

Ned Buntline (left), who almost singlehandedly created the legend of Buffalo Bill, appeared with the famous Indian scout (center) in a melodrama he wrote, *Scouts of the Plains* (1872). The third character, Texas Jack Omohundro (right), was also a real-life army scout whose exploits Buntline exaggerated. *(Library of Congress)*

Ned Buntline, whose real name was Edward Zane Carroll Judson, had a life almost as bizarre as the figures he wrote about. A Civil War deserter and bigamist when he was arrested in Tennessee for murder in 1846, Buntline escaped from his own lynching and fled to New York, where he wrote the first of some 400 Wild West adventures, 200 featuring the famous Indian scout Buffalo Bill.

In 1872, Buntline persuaded Buffalo Bill himself to appear in the first performance, in Chicago, of his new play, *Scouts of the Plains*. One reviewer called the play, in which the hero (played by author Ned Buntline) and heroine are rescued from death at the stake by Buffalo Bill's sharpshooting, "so wonderfully bad it is almost good." Neither for the first nor the last time, what the critics panned, the public loved: this first "western" was wildly popular. The success of *Scouts of the Plains* prompted Buffalo Bill to take command of his own stage career. Buffalo Bill's Wild West Show, featuring buffalo, Indians, former Indian scouts, and retired U.S. cavalrymen, first toured the country in 1883. Inventive posters showing what were described as "wily dusky warriors" performing "weird war dances" while they simultaneously attacked wagon trains, drew huge crowds. In 1885 both Chief Sitting Bull and the sharpshooter Annie Oakley joined the cast. Queen Victoria saw the show in London; the pope took in the spectacle at the Vatican; and 6 million saw it during the course of the Chicago World's Fair of 1893.

In the early years of the 20th century, motion pictures began to threaten the continued success of touring stage shows such as Buffalo Bill's Wild West Show. Like Ned Buntline's play *Scouts of the Plains*, one of the first successful movies was a western: *The Great Train Robbery* of 1909. Just as Buntline had inspired Buffalo Bill to start his own Wild West show, this first motion picture western persuaded him to try his hand at the new entertainment medium. Buffalo Bill's epic *The Indian Wars Refought*—with many battles filmed where they had taken place on the Great Plains—opened at movie theaters in 1913. In a tragedy almost as great as the loss of much of Catlin's Indian Gallery, only the last reel of the film has survived.

Buffalo Bill's *Indian Wars Refought* was the first of the hundreds of "cowboy and Indian" and "winning of the West" movies that dominated American moviemaking well into the 1940s and created a lasting image of the American West and the Plains Indian. In these movies, the hero is always the cowboy or cavalryman. John Ford's trilogy about the U.S. cavalry during the Plains Indian Wars—*Fort Apache* (1948), *She Wore a Yellow Ribbon* (1949), and *Rio Grande* (1950)—starred John Wayne who, along with Gary Cooper, was the best-known western film actor of the 1940s and 1950s.

In John Ford's westerns—perhaps especially in *She Wore a Yellow Ribbon,* which views Custer's defeat at Little Bighorn as a great American

Typical of the condescending treatment Native Americans received for many years is this World War II photograph of a Menominee chief in training for the U.S. Navy but posed with his feathered headdress. *(National Archives)*

tragedy—Indians may be portrayed as "noble savages," but never as heroes. All that began to change in 1950, with *Broken Arrow*, in which Jeff Chandler gives a sympathetic portrayal of the Apache leader Cochise. Then, in 1971, *Little Big Man*, starring Dustin Hoffman, not only portrayed the Sioux sympathetically but had a decidedly unsympathetic portrait of longtime American hero George Armstrong Custer. In 1990, *Dances with Wolves's* uncritically sympathetic presentation of life among the Lakota during the Plains Indian Wars earned the film an Oscar for best picture of the year.

Not surprisingly, movies like *Broken Arrow, Little Big Man,* and *Dances with Wolves* reflected a change in the attitudes of non-Indian Americans toward Native Americans. Beginning with the "Indian New Deal" of the 1930s, the U.S. government began to advocate Indian self-determination; by the 1960s, many of the rights of self-government and choice previously stripped from the Indians were reinstated. Change has been slow. Despite receiving citizenship in 1924, many Indians, like African Americans, were in fact denied the vote into the 1960s. Furthermore, it was not until 1978 that the American Indian

Making Amends
THE NATIONAL MUSEUM OF
THE AMERICAN INDIAN

IN 1989 CONGRESS PASSED AN ACT ESTABLISHING THE Smithsonian's National Museum of the American Indian, dedicated to the "preservation, study, and exhibition of the life, languages, literature, history, and arts of Native Americans." The museum's founding director, W. Richard West, is himself a member of the Cheyenne and Arapaho tribes of Oklahoma. The museum's website states that the museum's main facility is scheduled to open in 2004 on the historic Mall in Washington, D.C. Already, the museum's collection contains more than 1 million objects, with some 70 percent from North America and the rest from Mexico and Central and South America. The museum's goals are not static: There are plans to continue to collect objects, including artwork by contemporary Native American craftspeople and artists. At the same time, some sacred objects held by the museum are being returned to the tribes from which they were taken. As the museum's mission statement says, the museum will work "in consultation, collaboration, and cooperation with Natives . . . to protect, support, and enhance the development, maintenance, and perpetuation of Native culture and community." The museum's websites (www.americanindian.si.edu and www.nmai.si.edu) have detailed information on museum holdings and feature virtual exhibits. Six miles from Washington, D.C., in Suitland, Maryland, the Cultural Resources Center contains the museum's extensive archival and library collection and welcomes "scholars and non-scholars." The museum's third facility, the George Gustav Heye Center, is located in the historic Alexander Hamilton U.S. Custom House in Lower Manhattan. Although it is only

Freedom of Religion Act guaranteed Indians the right to practice their own religions.

During the 1960s, American Indians, along with other minority groups, began to embrace ethnic power and pride movements. The American Indian Movement (AIM), founded in 1968, was one of the first organizations to advocate "red power." Probably the best-known members of AIM were the Anishinabe (Ojibway) leader Dennis Banks a few blocks away from the former site of the World Trade Center, the Heye Center suffered only modest structural damage in the terrorist attack of September 11, 2001. At present, the Heye Center's strong suit is its Resource Center, where visitors can use a bank of computers to access information on the museum's holdings and on a broad range of American Indian history and contemporary life. The National Museum of the American Indian is the country's most important symbol of the current focus among American Indians to reclaim their past and shape their future.

The National Museum of the American Indian, located in the Alexander Hamilton U.S. Custom House in Lower Manhattan *(Photo courtesy of the National Museum of the American Indian, Smithsonian Institution)*

and the Oglala Lakota Yankton Dakota Russell Means, both active in the Indian takeover of Alcatraz Island in 1969. AIM suggested that Alcatraz, a former prison, should become a reservation and issued a tongue-in-cheek manifesto pointing out that the island was "more than suitable for an Indian Reservation as determined by the white man's own standards." For one thing, the manifesto stated, Alcatraz had "no fresh running water" and its "population has always been held as prisoners."

In 1973 and 1975, AIM activists occupied the Pine Ridge Reservation, the site of Wounded Knee, to protest what they perceived as the complicity of certain of the Sioux leaders—inevitably nicknamed "Uncle Tomahawks"—in those U.S. government policies that AIM thought harmful. When the government sent in federal agents, AIM maintained that this violated the Indian political sovereignty over the reservation guaranteed by the Treaty of Fort Laramie (1868). Ultimately, AIM leaders Leonard Peltier and Dennis Banks were both arrested, and Banks was briefly imprisoned while Peltier was sent to prison after being convicted of the murder of two FBI agents during the confrontation.

In the 1980s and 1990s, Native American activism has focused on promoting Indian rights and emphasizing the need for the Indians to reclaim their heritage. The National Museum of the American Indian (NMAI), with branches in New York and Washington, D.C., has worked closely with Native Americans on issues involving the proper treatment of Indian artifacts. Many items, such as sacred medicine bundles, have been returned by museums to the tribes from which they were taken. The NMAI has published *Native Peoples Magazine* (www.nativepeoples.com) since 1988. In addition, the works of talented Indian writers, such as Pulitzer Prize–winner N. Scott Momaday and Vine Deloria, whose *Custer Died for Your Sins* (1969) was a scathing indictment of government policy towards the Indians, gained widespread popularity.

In 1890, the year of Wounded Knee, the U.S. Census Bureau recorded only 237,196 Indians. It was not until 1917 that Indian births exceeded Indian deaths, and tribal numbers began slowly to increase. By 1990, the U.S. census listed 1.9 million Indians—an increase of nearly 140 percent since the 1970 census. The 2000 census listed 2,475,956 American Indians and Alaska Natives and 4,119,301 Americans of American Indian or Alaska Native and one or more other racial backgrounds. The total U.S. population in 2000 was 281,421,906. Interestingly New York was the city with the largest American Indian and Alaska Native population (41,289).

Opinions differ as to how to interpret this vigorous growth in Indian population. Some have spoken of a "*Dances with Wolves* syndrome" that makes it fashionable to claim Native American heritage. Others have pointed out that the current spirit of multiculturalism in America makes it comfortable to declare a nonwhite heritage. Still others have suggested that the considerable economic benefits available to those who can prove membership in several recently prosperous casino-owning tribes may tempt the unscrupulous to attempt to claim Indian heritage.

It has now been more than 100 years since the last Lakota surrendered after Wounded Knee. The American psychiatrist and scholar Erik Erikson wrote that the Plains Indians after Wounded Knee were "warriors without weapons." Erikson attributed many of the problems of the 20th-century Plains Indians, including chronic unemployment and endemic alcoholism, to the fact that a people who for generations roamed the Great Plains lost their way of life virtually overnight and could not adapt to the new life thrust upon them by the whites.

For now, the rebirth of Indian culture gives grounds for cautious optimism that Native Americans are reclaiming the heritage that once seemed lost in the last days of the Plains Indian Wars. Perhaps the enormous head of the Lakota hero Crazy Horse that is being carved high on one of the sacred Black Hills of South Dakota, not far from the busts of Washington, Jefferson, Lincoln, and Theodore Roosevelt on Mount Rushmore, is as good a symbol as any of the way in which the Plains Indians are reclaiming their heritage and taking their place in an increasingly multicultural America.

Glossary

adobe   A mixture of straw and clay that, when shaped into bricks and baked in the sun, was used by the Indians of the Southwest (including the Hopi and Zuni) to build homes and walls, especially those often called pueblos (Spanish for "village"). Sometimes the word is used alone to mean "house."

ambush   A surprise attack made from a hiding place.

amulet   A small object, often worn around the neck, and intended as a charm against evil or injury.

annuity   A yearly payment in money or in goods for services or property. The U.S. government often paid little or none of the agreed-upon annuities to the Plains Indians for relinquishing their lands.

archaeology   The study of the past through material remains, including buildings, objects of household and artistic interest (such as pottery), and plant and animal remains.

artillery   A division of the U.S. Army that uses large, crew-operated weapons such as cannons and missiles; the term is used to describe both the weapons and the army unit using them.

assimilation   The process by which a minority group adopts, willingly or under pressure, the customs and attitudes of the majority among whom they live.

barbed wire   A double strand of twisted wire with hooks, or barbs, invented in 1873 and used by early settlers to make fences to protect their farmland from the widely ranging cattle and sheep that grazed freely on the Great Plains; later used for defensive fencing on the battlefield.

barrack   A building used to house soldiers; usually the largest building in a frontier fort.

buckskin   The skin of a male deer, used to make leather clothing.

bustle   A small pad or frame worn underneath the back of a woman's skirt; it was regarded as highly fashionable between about 1860 and 1880.

Caucasoid   A member of the racial division (sometimes called Caucasian) which includes peoples now found mainly in Europe, northern Africa, western Asia, India, and North and South America. The name is based on their assumed original homeland, the Caucasus Mountains in Russia, Georgia, and Armenia. They share various primary biological factors and secondary physical characteristics.

cavalry   During the 19th century, the division of an army and its personnel who moved about on horseback and usually fought on horseback; in the 20th century the cavalry began to use motorized vehicles, eventually including helicopters.

chip   A piece of dried animal dung burnt as a fuel.

civilization   The culture of a people, or geographical location, or specific period of time; often used to imply the possession of skills such as writing which other cultures, such as those of most American Indians at the time of conquest, did not possess.

coup count   The term used to describe the widespread practice among Native Americans of gaining honor by touching but not killing an enemy in battle, often with a special instrument called the coup stick (from the French for "touch").

DNA   (deoxyribonucleic acid)   The nucleic acid found in all cells and which contains the organism's genetic information; because it is so distinctive, it can be used to trace an individual's line of descent.

fort   A fortified camp, building, or complex of buildings used for military purposes.

frontier   A term used variously to describe the boundary between one country and another and to suggest the undeveloped land beyond habitation; the term is also used metaphorically, as in the "new frontier," to suggest an unexplored area of intellectual or social possibilities.

Gatling gun   A rapid-fire gun, invented in 1862 by Richard Gatling, with numerous rotating barrels (often called a machine gun) that could fire up to 600 rounds a minute.

Great Spirit   The most common English translation of a multitude of names used by many American Indians to describe their most powerful deity.

hippophagist A humorously coined word based on the Greek for "horse-eater."

"Indian problem" A term used by private citizens and the U.S. government, especially in the 19th century, to describe the presence of American Indians on land desired by settlers.

infantry Those members of the military who fight on foot.

immigrant A person who moves to any country from another country with the intention of residing in the new country.

legend A story, usually handed down from generation to generation and generally believed to be true, although unverifiable in most of its details.

Medal of Honor The United States highest military honor, established by a joint Act of Congress in 1862. During the Indian Campaigns (1861–91) 242 medals were awarded for heroism; as of February 2002, 3,456 of these medals have been awarded.

migration The act of moving from one place to another. Although now usually used to describe animals, such as buffalo, which move from one feeding place to another at different times of the year, it is also used to refer to the major relocations by Indian tribes.

missionaries Individuals who undertake religious work, usually in remote or foreign areas, and often with the goal of converting those they encounter. The early Spanish and French Catholic missionaries in America established a string of missions with churches and schools to educate Native Americans and convert them from their own religious beliefs to Christianity.

Mongoloid A member of the racial division (sometimes called Mongolian) including peoples now found mainly in central, eastern, and southeastern Asia. The name is based on one of their basic population groups, the Mongols. Mongoloids share various primary biological factors and secondary physical characteristics.

myth A story, usually of great antiquity, about ancestors, demigods, spirits, and deities, that expresses profound beliefs about the world.

nomads People who do not live permanently in one place but move from place to place, usually following a seasonal pattern; most of the Plains Indians led a nomadic life before the Europeans arrived in the west.

Oliver chilled plow   An iron plow, patented in 1868 by James Oliver, made by an innovative process that chilled the molten iron rapidly, giving its cutting blade enormous strength and revolutionizing farming in the 19th century.

pemmican   Sun-dried meat, usually buffalo or venison, that was mixed with fat and kept indefinitely; a popular, easily portable, food of the Plains Indians.

pictograph   An image, either painted, drawn, or carved, that represents an object, sound, or word. Pictographs were widely used among the Plains Indians, often in narrative accounts on stones or buffalo and deer hide.

prairie   Any large, basically flat, essentially treeless stretch of often arid grassland; often used specifically of the Great Plains in the interior of the United States.

Praying Indians   A general term used by Europeans and Americans for Native Americans who converted to Christianity; in the 17th century, the Native Americans of Massachusetts were encouraged to live in what were known as "Praying towns."

proclamation   A statement or decision that is announced or published, usually officially. It was Lincoln's Emancipation Proclamation (1863) that freed the slaves.

prospector   Someone who looks for something; usually used of the person who searches for gold and other precious metals or soil.

regiment   A unit of military personnel of flexible number, usually made up of two battalions; each battalion is usually made up of two or more companies.

reparations   The act, often involving payment, of making amends, or equalizing a situation, particularly after a war. The Plains Indians were often promised reparations for their land.

reservation   Land set aside by the federal government for the exclusive use of Native Americans.

scalp   The skin on top of the head. When that skin was removed, with or without the hair, it served as a trophy or as proof of the death of the human or animal scalped; in fact, some people did survive being scalped if no damage was done to the brain.

scout   A skilled tracker or sentry who could find signs of human or animal behavior and existence in a multitude of signs (footprints, campfires, and the like); often associated with military spying or information gathering.

scurvy   A disease caused by a lack of vitamin C; it was widespread among people who did not eat many fresh fruits.

settlement   A small group of people (settlers) and their homes and other buildings; often used of such communities on the frontier, or in newly colonized land, although it can also be used of small communities of the original inhabitants in a land undergoing settlement by immigrants.

shaman   A priestlike figure, believed by others (usually in his tribe) to have magical powers and the ability to mediate between the real world and the spirit world; sometimes used as a synonym for medicine man.

sideshow   A term usually applied to the less important act or acts with a circus; used metaphorically to describe any diversion from the main issue.

smallpox   A virulent, very contagious, often fatal illness, accompanied by high fever and pus-filled sores; now eliminated throughout the world, it was one of the leading causes of death for Native Americans when first exposed to it by Europeans.

sod   Grass-covered soil held together by matted roots; when cut and dug up in blocks, it could be used to make quite durable houses.

squaw   A corruption of the Native American word for woman or wife; often used by European Americans in a dismissive or deprecatory fashion. Considered offensive.

steamship   A ship whose engine produced steam and water that propelled its rudders or paddles; steamboats modeled on those designed by Robert Fulton (the first in 1807) journeyed up and down the Mississippi and Missouri Rivers at the time of the Plains Indians Wars.

stockade   A wooden or earthen protective fence around settlement or military site; sometimes used to refer to the fortified jail within a fort or settlement.

stampede   A mad dash by humans or animals; sometimes used as a hunting technique by Native Americans, who would stampede buffalo over a cliff or into a corral.

suffragist   A word derived from *suffrage* (the right to vote); historically *suffragists* applied to those who from the mid-1800s on worked to gain women the right to vote.

sweat ceremony A ritual purification practiced by men among the Plains Indians tribes to gain courage and by men and women for reasons of health; the ceremony took place in a sweat lodge, a kind of sauna, where water poured over hot stones produced steam.

telegraph A system of communicating by transmitting letters and numbers through wires by electrical impulses.

territory An administrative unit of land, such as the Northwest Territory, usually headed by a governor. Most territories later achieved statehood. At present, Guam, the Virgin Islands, and American Samoa are administered as U.S. territories.

treaty A formal agreement between governments or interested parties to formalize an agreement. Treaties between the U.S. government and the Plains Indians consistently diminished first the Indians' original homelands and later their reservations.

travois A French-Canadian name for the device used by some Plains Indians to convey their possessions when on the move. It is a frame slung between two poles that are pulled by a horse or dog.

tribe A group usually linked by heritage, language, culture, and dwelling places.

vision A visual perception of a supernatural being or episode; as a mystical or spiritual experience, it is an important component of most religions, including those of the Plains Indians.

warpath A slang term, first used by those who were not Native Americans, to describe hostile Indians; now used metaphorically of anyone on the attack.

warrior A military combatant, usually male; the term is used by anthropologists to characterize entire societies as "warrior societies."

wet nurse A woman who nurses a child who is not her own.

Further Reading

NONFICTION

Andrist, Ralph K. *The Long Death: The Last Days of the Plains Indian.* New York: Macmillan, 1964.

Bancroft-Hunt, Norman, and Werner Forman. *The Indian of the Great Plains.* New York: Peter Bedrick Books, 1989.

Bancroft-Hunt, Norman. *Warriors: Warfare and the Native American Indian.* London: Salamander Books, 1995.

Berkhofer, Robert F. *The White Man's Indian.* New York: Alfred A. Knopf, 1978.

Blaisdell, Bob, ed. *Great Speeches by Native Americans.* Mineola, N.Y.: Dover Thrift Edition, 2000.

Bordewich, Fergus M. *Killing the White Man's Indian: Reinventing Native Americans at the End of the Twentieth Century.* New York: Doubleday, 1996.

Brown, Dee. *Bury My Heart at Wounded Knee: An Indian History of the American West.* New York: Henry Holt, 1970.

Bruchac, Joseph. *Sacajawea.* New York: Harcourt, 2000.

Carter, Samuel. *Cherokee Sunset: A Nation Betrayed.* Garden City, N.Y.: Doubleday, 1976.

Connell, Evan S. *Son of the Morning Star: Custer and the Little Bighorn.* New York: Harper & Row, 1984.

DeLoria, Philip, and Neal Salisbury. *A Companion to American Indian History.* Malden, Mass.: Blackwell Publishers, 2001.

Deloria, Vine, Jr. *Behind the Trail of Broken Promises.* New York: Delacorte Press, 1974.

———. *Custer Died for Your Sins.* New York: Macmillan, 1969.

Dewar, Elaine. *Bones: Discovering the First Americans.* New York: Carroll & Graf, 2002.

Eastman, Elaine Goodale. *Sister to the Sioux.* Lincoln: University of Nebraska Press, 1978.

Ewers, John C. *Plains Indian History and Culture.* Norman: University of Oklahoma Press, 1997.

FURTHER READING

Faulk, Odie B. *The Geronimo Campaign.* New York: Oxford University Press, 1969.

Fehrenbach, T. R. *Comanches: The Destruction of a Nation.* New York: Knopf, 1974.

Flood, Renee Sanson. *Lost Bird of Wounded Knee.* New York: Scribner, 1995.

Frazier, Ian. *On the Rez.* New York: Farrar, Straus & Giroux, 2000.

Gray, John S. *Centennial Campaign: The Sioux War of 1876.* Norman: University of Oklahoma Press, 1976.

Greene, Jerome A. *Lakota and Cheyenne: Indian Views of the Great Sioux War, 1876–1877.* Norman: University of Oklahoma Press, 1995.

Grinnell, George Bird. *The Fighting Cheyennes.* North Dighton, Mass.: J. G. Press, 1975.

Haley, James A. *Apaches.* Garden City, N.Y.: Doubleday, 1981.

———. *The Buffalo War: The History of the Red River Indian Uprising of 1874.* Garden City, N.Y.: Doubleday, 1976.

Hampton, Bruce. *Children of Grace: The Nez Perce War of 1877.* New York: Henry Holt, 1994.

Hardorff, Richard G. *Lakota Recollections of the Custer Fight: New Sources of Indian-Military History.* Lincoln: University of Nebraska Press, 1991.

Heat Moon, William Least. *River Horse.* New York: Penguin, 2001.

Hungry Wolf, Beverly. *The Ways of My Grandmothers.* New York: Quill, 1982.

Josephy, Alvin M., Jr. *The Indian Heritage Book of America.* Boston: Houghton Mifflin, 1991.

———. *Red Power: The American Indians' Fight for Freedom.* New York: American Heritage Press, 1971.

Manzione, Joseph. *I Am Looking to the North for my Life: Sitting Bull, 1876–1881.* Salt Lake City: University of Utah Press, 1991.

McDermott, John D. *A Guide to the Indian Wars of the West.* Lincoln: University of Nebraska, 1998.

McLuhan, T. C. *Dream Tracks: The Railroad and the American Indian 1890–1930.* New York: Harry N. Abrams, 1985.

Mitchell, Emerson Blackhorse, and T. D. Allen. *Miracle Hill: The Story of a Navajo Boy.* Norman: University of Oklahoma Press, 1967.

Moquin, Wayne, and Charles Van Doren eds. *Great Documents in American Indian History.* New York: Praeger, 1973.

Nabokov, Peter. *Native American Testimony.* New York: Viking Penguin, 1991.

Niethammer, Carolyn. *Daughters of the Earth: The Lives and Legends of American Indian Women.* New York: Macmillan, 1977.

Peters, Virginia Bergman. *Women of the Earth Lodges: Tribal Life on the Plains.* Norman: University of Oklahoma Press, 1995.

Prucha, Francis Paul. *The Churches and the Indian Schools, 1888–1912.* Lincoln: University of Nebraska Press, 1979.

Reedstrom, E. Lisle. *Apache Wars: An Illustrated Battle History.* New York: Sterling Publishing, 1990.

Remini, Robert V. *Andrew Jackson and His Indian Wars.* New York: Viking Press, 2001.

Roberts, David. *Once They Moved Like the Wind: Cochise, Geronimo, and the Apache Wars.* New York: Simon and Schuster, 1993.

Robinson, Charles M. *A Good Year to Die: The Story of the Great Sioux War.* Norman: University of Oklahoma Press, 1995.

Sajna, Mike. *Crazy Horse.* New York: John Wiley, 2000.

Sandoz, Mari. *The Battle of Little Bighorn.* Lincoln: University of Nebraska, 1978.

Schultz, Duane. *Month of the Freezing Moon: The Sand Creek Massacre of November 1864.* New York: St. Martin's Press, 1990.

Standing Bear, Luther. *My People the Sioux.* Boston: Houghton Mifflin, 1928.

Stands in Timber, John, and Margot Liberty. *Cheyenne Memories.* New Haven, Conn.: Yale University Press, 1967.

Turner, Frederick Jackson. *The Frontier in American History.* New York: Holt, 1920.

Tillett, Leslie, ed. *Wind on the Buffalo Grass: The Indians' Own Account of the Battle of the Little Bighorn.* New York: Thomas Cromwell, 1976.

Trafzer, Clifford E. *The Kit Carson Campaign: The Last Great Navajo War.* Norman: University of Oklahoma, 1982.

Utley, Robert. *Frontier Regulars: The United States Army and the Indian, 1866–1891.* New York: Macmillan, 1973.

———. *The Lance and the Shield: The Life and Times of Sitting Bull.* New York: Holt, 1993.

———. *The Last Days of the Sioux Nation.* New Haven, Conn.: Yale University Press, 1963.

Vestal, Stanley. *Sitting Bull: Champion of the Sioux.* Norman: University of Oklahoma Press, 1932.

Wallace, Ernst, and E. Adamson Hoebel. *The Comanches, Lords of the South Plains.* Norman: University of Oklahoma, 1952.

Walton, George. *Fearless and Free: The Seminole Indian War, 1835–1842.* New York: Bobbs-Merrill, 1977.

FICTION

Berger, Thomas. *Little Big Man.* New York: Delta/Saint Lawrence Publishing, 1989.

Erdrich, Louise. *The Bingo Palace.* New York: HarperCollins, 1994.

McMurtry, Larry. *Buffalo Girls.* New York: Simon and Schuster, 1990.

Power, Susan. *The Grass Dancer.* New York: Putnam, 1994.

Silko, Leslie Marmon. *Ceremony.* New York: Viking Press, 1977.

————. *Gardens in the Dunes.* New York: Simon and Schuster, 2000.
Welch, James. *The Heartsong of Charging Elk.* New York: Doubleday, 2000.

WEBSITES

Index of Native American Resources on the Internet. Available online. www.hanksville.org/NAresources/. Downloaded on September 9, 2002.
Indianz.com. Available online. www.indianz.com. Downloaded on September 9, 2002.
John G. Neihardt Internet Project Chronology. Available online. URL: http://www.wayne.esu1.k12.ne.us/neihardt/chron.html. Downloaded on May 7, 2002.
Kennewick Man Virtual Interpretive Center. Available online. URL: http://www.kennewick-man.com. Downloaded on May 7, 2002.
NativeCulture.com. Available online. www.nativeculture.com. Downloaded on September 9, 2002.
Native Web: Resources for Indigenous Cultures Around the World. Available online. www.nativeweb.org. Downloaded on September 9, 2002.
Plains Indians—the Overland Trail Links. Available online. URL: http://www.over-land.com/indians.html. Downloaded on May 7, 2002.
Sioux Nation. Available online. www.crystalinks.com/sioux.html. Downloaded on September 9, 2002.
Techniques for Evaluating Native Indian Web Sites. Available online. www.u.arizona.edu/~ecubbins/webcrit.html. Downloaded on September 9, 2002.
"The Wars with the Plains Indians." On WWW-VL History: USA. Reconstruction. Available online. URL: www.ku.edu/history/VL/USA/ERAS/reconstruction.html#plains_indians. Downloaded on May 7, 2002.

Index

Page numbers in *italics* indicate a photograph. Page numbers followed by *m* indicate maps. Page numbers followed by *g* indicate glossary entries. Page numbers in **boldface** indicate box features.

INDEX

INDEX

INDEX

158

159

INDEX

INDEX

162

PLAINS INDIAN WARS

INDEX